Inn Love

••••••••••• *Pamela Lanier's* •••••••••••
RECIPES *for* ROMANCE

DEDICATED TO
*Juliet Dawn
and
Emilia Rose*

& THANKS

Senior Editor
Ashley Bolettieri

Assistant Editor
Jenny Juhl

Research Assistants
*Arlyn Silacci
Courtney Humiston*

And a very special thank you to designer Laura Lamar.

Special thanks to all of the team at Bed & Breakfast Inns and Guesthouses International, especially

Membership Director
*Shannon Holl,
and Nicole Day,
Steve Kelez,
Marie Lanier,
Bianca Licata, Melissa Miranda, Gini Rhoda, Vivian Sturdavant, and Staci van Wyk.*

Innkeeping is both a lifestyle and an avocation – innkeepers are in the frontlines of providing hospitality, comfort, and succor to weary travelers – well done!

The information in this book was supplied in large part by the inns themselves, and is subject to change without notice. We strongly recommend that you call ahead to verify the information presented here before making final plans or reservations. The author and publisher make no representation that this book is accurate or complete. Errors and omissions, whether typographical, clerical, or otherwise, may sometimes occur herein.

The information about the properties in this publication is intended for personal use only. Any and all commercial use of the information in this publication is strictly prohibited.

This book may not be reproduced in whole or in part in any form or by any means, electronic or mechanical, including photocopying, recording, or by any informtion storage and retrieval system now known or hereafter invented, without written permission from the publisher.

The images in this book are representive of the B&B lifestyle and cuisine, and do not exactly reflect the recipes in this book.

© 2012 by Lanier Publishing International, Ltd.
All rights reserved.
Published 2010.
ISBN 978-0-9654066-3-5

This book can be ordered by mail from the publisher. Please include $3.50 for postage and handling for each copy. But try your local bookstore first!

Lanier Publishing International, Ltd.
PO Box 2240
Petaluma, CA 94953
tel. 707.763.0271
fax. 707.763.5762
e-mail lanier@travelguides.com

Find us on the internet at:
www.LanierBB.com
www.TravelGuideS.com

Distributed to the book trade by:
National Book Network
15200 NBN Way, Bldg. B
Blue Ridge Summit, PA 21264-2188
website: nbnbooks.com
tel. 1-800-462-6420

Design by MAX DESIGN STUDIO.*net*
Vintage ilustrations from Karen's Whimsey & Dover

Inn Love

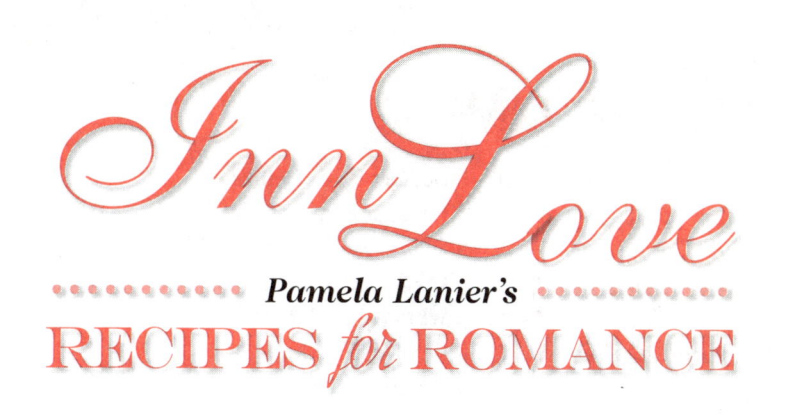

Pamela Lanier's
RECIPES *for* ROMANCE

*Romantic Getaways Coast to Coast
Plus Recipes You'll Both Love*

Bed and Breakfast Collection™
BY PAMELA LANIER

LANIER PUBLISHING INTERNATIONAL, LTD.
Petaluma, California

Contents

Gravity is not responsible for people falling in love.

ALBERT EINSTEIN

ii Dedication & Thanks
10 Introduction

A CONTINENTAL COURTSHIP

14 White Chocolate Cherry Scones
15 Breakfast Scones
16 Cranberry Orange Scones
17 White Chocolate Craisin Scones
18 Croissants a l'Orange
19 Savory Asparagus Croissant
20 Citrus Croissants
21 Almond Poppy Seed Muffins
22 Rhubarb-Pecan Muffins
23 Cranberry Orange Muffins
24 Triple Chocolate Banana Muffins
25 Cranberry Crunch Muffins
26 Sour Cream Blueberry Muffins
27 Sun-Dried Tomato and Feta Crown Muffins
28 Baked Oatmeal
29 Date Nut Bread
30 Blueberry Cream Cheese Casserole
31 Almond Raspberry Coffee Cake
32 Crumb Coffee Cake with Cream Cheese and Raspberry Topping
34 Cape Cod Cranberry Coffee Cake
36 Zucchini Carrot Coconut Macadamia Nut Bread

37 Rhubarb Bread
38 Orange Muffin Bread
39 Banana Cranberry Nut Bread
40 Tropical Blend Banana Bread
41 Raspberry-Cheese Coffee Cake

AN EGGS-TRAVAGANT AFFAIR

44 Baked Eggs Florentine
45 The Innkeeper's Souffle
46 Featherbed Eggs
47 Sourdough Eggs
48 Italian Sausage and Egg Casserole
49 Sunrise Service Egg Dish
50 Eggs Florentine
    with Asiago Cheese
51 Green Chile Cheese Puff
52 Eggs Florentine
53 Grits Soufflé
54 Spinach Omelet Roll
55 Southwestern Frittata
56 Vegetable Frittata/Strata
58 Smoked Salmon Strata
59 Spinach-Sausage Quiche
60 Smokey Cheddar and Bacon Quiche
61 Jen's Basic Quiche
62 Avocado Quiche
63 Wine Country Quiche
64 Quiche Havarti

Love conquers all.

VIRGIL

Contents

65 Crustless Salmon Quiche
66 Spinach and Mushroom Quiche

SWEETHEART SUNRISE

70 Strawberry Cheese Crepe
71 Filling for Bananas Foster Crepes
72 Peach and Blueberry Breakfast Pie
73 Mökki Pannukakku
   (Finnish Cottage Pancake)
74 Hot Buttered Rum Sauce
75 Baked Whole Wheat Raspberry Pancakes
76 Apple Crisp Pancake
77 Lemon-Lovers Ricotta Pancakes
78 Dutch Pancakes
79 Outrageous French Toast
80 Cheesecake-Stuffed Raspberry French Toast
81 Raspberry Stuffed French Toast
82 Candy Apple French Toast
83 Berry Good French Toast
84 Cranberry-Almond French Toast Souffle
85 Orange Blossom French Toast
86 Carmel Apple French Toast
87 "Temptation" Apple Baked French Toast
88 Crème Brulee French Toast
89 Stuffed French Toast

If you want to be loved, be lovable.

OVID

90   Baked French Toast
91   Honey Baked French Toast
92   Holiday Morning French Toast
93   Wild Rice Waffles

ENTICING SIDE DISHES

96   Berry Cooler
97   Carmelized Bacon
98   Strawberry Rhubarb Compote
99   Candied Walnuts
100 Chilled Creamy Peach Soup
101 Strawberry Balsamic Soup
102 Broccoli Potato Soup
103 Lucy's French Onion Soup
104 Three Cheese Creamy Champagne Broccoli Soup
106 Gingered Fruit Salad
107 Fruit Salade Vinaigrette
108 Garlic Herb Vinaigrette
109 Romaine Orange Salad
110 Fresh Pineapple Ambrosia
111 Spinach Parmesan
112 Summer Squash

ALLURING APPETIZERS

116 Cheese Straws
117 Pear, Walnut and Blue Cheese Flat Bread
118 Baked Wonton Cups

The hunger for love is much more difficult to remove than the hunger for bread.

MOTHER TERESA

Contents

- 119 Charleston Chutney Cheese Appetizer
- 120 Caper Puffs
- 121 Chocolate Chip Pumpkin Bread
- 122 Crab Cakes with Charred Corn, Tomato Salsa, and Poblano Aioli

THE MAIN SQUEEZE
- 126 Shirley's Stuffed Pork Loin with Chutney
- 128 Seared Duck with Risotto and Brussels Sprouts
- 130 Chicken with Five Herb Cream Sauce
- 132 Ahi Tuna Provencal
- 133 Seafood Risotto
- 134 Trout Hugo

SWEET NOTHINGS
- 138 Saskatoon Pie
- 139 Raspberry Walnut Torte
- 140 Sumptuous Apple Crisp
- 141 Apple Cranberry Crisp
- 142 Strawberry Bavarian Charlotte
- 144 Bourbon Pecan Pie
- 145 Rhubarb Torte
- 146 Gifford Family Tart
- 147 Cherry-Berry on a Cloud
- 148 Bread Pudding with Sweet Bread
- 149 Poached Peaches with White Cheese Mousse

I can live without money, but I cannot live without love.

JUDY GARLAND

150 Strawberries with Lemon Creme
151 Dipped Cornbread
with Fruit and Creme
152 Poached Peaches
in Champagne
153 Apple Dumplings
154 Passionate Poached
Pears in Raspberry Sauce
155 Cherry Cheesecake
156 Pumpkin Cheesecake
157 Overnight Pear Souffle
158 Chocolate Creme Brulée
159 Apple Claflutti
160 Pear Ginger Upside-Down Cake
161 Camp Fire Pineapple Upside Down Cake
162 Almond Pear Clafouti
163 West Haven Cake
164 Chocolate Sherry Cake
165 Zucchini Chocolate Cake
166 Bittersweet Chocolate Fondue
167 Lemon Almond Biscotti
168 Chocolate Mint Sticks
169 Welsh Cakes
170 Chocolate Melt-Away Cookies
171 White Lace Inn Cookies
172 Sweet Treats

174 INDEX
Alphabetical Listing of Inns and B&Bs

Introduction

> *Your words are my food, your breath my wine. You are everything to me.*
>
> SARAH BERNHARDT

COURTING COUPLES, honeymooners, and longtime lovers have long enjoyed not only the comforts of bed and breakfast inns worldwide, but the delicious family recipes they feature, too. Passed down through generations and perfected through time, these recipes add the ideal touch to any weekend escape. From the savory to the sweet, innkeepers around the globe share with guests not just an appetizing menu, but also a piece of their heart. Paired with a cultured atmosphere and personal details, these elegant bed and breakfast meals set the stage for you and your loved one to create long lasting memories. Here, from the soul of Canada to the depths of America's heartland, innkeepers provide you with some of their favorite cuisines. Bring romance to your table with these traditional recipes from some of the finest innkeepers Canada and the United States have to offer.

BON APPÉTIT!
Pamela Lanier

11

A Continental Courtship

REMEMBER YOUR FIRST WEEKEND away together? A leisurely continental breakfast completed by your favorite muffin, scone or morning bread. Fresh squeezed juice and a great cup of coffee. A gorgeous view, a comfortable seat, and that gentle warmth growing between the two of you. How wonderful would it be to gaze across your breakfast table and transform it into that delectable repast? So why not do just that? Put your busy life on hold, and dive into the meal that brought you two together. Rekindle those feelings in your own kitchen with these heartwarming dishes. All you need is one of these fabulous recipes and someone you love to share them with.

> *There is too little courtship in the world.*
>
> VERNON LEE

A Continental Courtship

ABBEYMOORE MANOR

White Chocolate Cherry Scones

Abbeymoore Manor
1470 Rockland Ave
Victoria, BC
250-370-1470
www.abbeymoore.com
innkeeper@abbeymoore.com

INGREDIENTS:
2½ cups all-purpose flour

2 tbsp sugar

2½ tsp baking powder

1/2 tsp baking soda

1/2 tsp salt

1/2 cup cold butter, cubed

1 cup buttermilk

1 egg

1 cup dried cherries

3 oz chopped white chocolate

TOPPING:
2 oz melted white chocolate

INSTRUCTIONS:
Line baking sheet with parchment paper, set aside. Preheat oven to 400 degrees F or 200 degrees C.

In large bowl, whisk together flour, sugar, baking powder, baking soda and salt. Using your hands, blend the butter until the mixture resembles coarse crumbs. In small bowl, whisk buttermilk with egg, add to flour mixture. Sprinkle with cherries and white chocolate, stir mixture with fork to make soft dough. With lightly floured hands press dough into ball. On floured surface, knead dough a few times but do not over knead. Pat dough out to thickness desired and cut with cutter *(I use a glass)*.

Bake for approximately 15 to 18 minutes. Transfer to rack and let cool. Drizzle with chocolate and let stand approx 1 hour. Can be frozen if wrapped individually and stored in airtight container. Makes from 12 to 15 scones depending on cutter size used.

COOK TIME: *15 min*
YIELD: *12 servings*

THE MARIA ATWOOD INN'S
Breakfast Scones

INSTRUCTIONS:
The night before mix dry ingredients together in a medium size bowl. The next morning add buttermilk, butter Crisco, egg, flavoring, and nuts and/or fruit. Stir together, gently kneading to complete mixing ingredients. Shape into a large ball and flatten into a circle on a cookie sheet or baking stone. Score into 8 pieces with serrated knife. Another method is to make individual scones by shaping them into small balls (no need to flatten) and placing on the sheet or stone. Bake at 350 degrees F for 18 to 22 minutes, until lightly browned and toothpick comes out clear. Serve warm with butter, honey, jam, or flavored cream cheese. ENJOY!

COOK TIME: *20 min*
YIELD: *10 servings*

The Maria Atwood Inn
71 Hill Rd, Rt#3A
Franklin, NH
603-934-3666
www.atwoodinn.com
info@atwoodinn.com

INGREDIENTS:

2¼ cups flour

1/2 cup sugar

2 tsp baking powder

1/2 tsp baking soda

1/4 tsp salt

1/2 cup buttermilk

1/2 cup butter Crisco shortening

1 egg

1 tsp flavoring (vanilla, orange, or maple)

1/2 cup nuts of choice (walnuts, pecans, or hazelnuts)

1/2 cup fruit of choice (blueberry, cranberry, dates, or raisins) *(if using only nuts or fruit alone should total 1 cup)*

A Continental Courtship

HILL FARM INN

Cranberry Orange Scones

Hill Farm Inn
458 Hill Farm Rd
Arlington, VT
802-375-2269
www.hillfarminn.com
stay@hillfarminn.com

INGREDIENTS:

3 cups all purpose flour

1/3 cup sugar

2½ tsp baking powder

1 tsp salt

1/2 tsp baking soda

1 tbsp grated orange peel

3/4 cup (1½ sticks) chilled unsalted butter, cut into 1/2-inch pieces

3/4 cup dried cranberries

1 cup chilled buttermilk, well shaken

INSTRUCTIONS:
Preheat oven to 375 degrees F.

Measure flour, then sift into large bowl with sugar, baking powder, salt and baking soda. Mix in orange peel.

Add butter and cut with pastry cutter or rub with fingertips until mixture resembles coarse meal. Mix in dried cranberries.

Gradually add buttermilk, tossing with fork until moist clumps form. Turn dough out onto lightly floured work surface. Knead briefly to bind dough, about 4 turns. Using lightly floured hands, form into ovals about 2" × 3½" × 1".

Bake on baking sheet lined with parchment paper until tops are golden brown, about 25 minutes. Let stand on baking sheet 10 minutes. Serve warm. Makes about 12 scones.

COOK TIME: *25 min*
YIELD: *1 dozen*

16 *Inn Love*

A.G. THOMSON HOUSE

White Chocolate Craisin Scones

INSTRUCTIONS:
Mix dry ingredients. Cut in butter then add the chocolate chips and craisins. Mix in wet ingredients just until blended. Lightly knead until mixed. Do not over-mix. Place on a lightly buttered cookie sheet. Score into 8 pieces.

NOTE: *I don't take the dough out of the bowl. I knead it in the bowl and lay it out on a baking sheet, then flatten into a circle. I score the dough instead of cutting all the way through. This is just an easier and faster way for me – do what works best for you.*

Sprinkle with granulated or raw sugar. Bake 15–20 minutes at 375 degrees F or until golden brown.

COOK TIME: *15–20 min*
YIELD: *8 servings*

INGREDIENTS:
2 cups flour

1/3 cup sugar

2 tsp baking powder

1/2 tsp salt

1/4 cup butter

1/2 cup heavy cream

1 egg

1½ tsp vanilla

6 oz white chocolate chips

1/2 cup craisins

A.G. Thomson House
2617 E Third St
Duluth, MN
218-724-3464
www.thomsonhouse.biz
info@thomsonhouse.biz

A Continental Courtship

THE MAINSTAY INN

Croissants a l'Orange

INGREDIENTS:

6 croissants

1 (9 oz) jar orange marmalade

3 oz orange juice

5 eggs

1 cup heavy cream

1 tsp almond extract

strawberries for garnish

canned or fresh Mandarin orange sections for garnish

INSTRUCTIONS:

Cut croissants in half lengthwise and place bottom halves in buttered 12×9-inch oven-proof dish. Thin marmalade with orange juice and spoon over each bottom half, saving a little to be used as a glaze. Replace croissant tops. Beat eggs, cream and almond extract. Pour over top of the croissants. Spoon some thinned marmalade over top. Soak overnight.

Remove from fridge 45 minutes before baking. Bake in a preheated oven 350 degrees for about 25 minutes. Serve hot and garnish with strawberries and Mandarin orange sections.

COOK TIME: *25 min*
YIELD: *6 servings*

All happiness depends on a leisurely breakfast.

JOHN GUNTHER

The Mainstay Inn
635 Columbia Ave
Cape May, NJ
609-884-8690
www.mainstayinn.com
mainstayinn@comcast.net

Inn Love

CAPE CHARLES HOUSE B&B

Savory Asparagus Croissant

INSTRUCTIONS:

Slice croissants in half, crosswise and lay bottom half of the croissant in 9×12-inch baking dish, that has been sprayed lightly with Pam.

Prepare each croissant by layering as follows: a slice of Swiss cheese, 4 asparagus spears, sprinkle with Parmesan cheese, garlic salt, black pepper, nutmeg and dill weed, ending with another slice of Swiss cheese. In a separate bowl, combine the eggs, mustard, half & half and cayenne pepper. Take the top half of the croissant and quickly immerse in the egg mixture and place it on top of the assembled croissant bottom. Pour the remaining egg mixture over all the croissants. Sprinkle with sesame seeds over all.

Bake at 350 degrees F for 30 minutes, or until custard is set. To serve, cut around each croissant and use a spatula to transfer to serving plate.

NOTE: *This can be made ahead. After completely assembled, cover with foil and refrigerate overnight. Bring to room temperature: uncover and leave on counter for 15 minutes before baking.*

COOK TIME: *30 min*
YIELD: *4 servings*

INGREDIENTS:

16 asparagus spears

4 baked croissants

8 slices Swiss cheese

1/4 cup Parmesan cheese

1¼ cup half & half

4 eggs

1/2 tsp ground nutmeg

1 tsp dill weed

cracked pepper

1 tsp Grey Poupon mustard

1/2 tsp garlic salt

1/8 tsp cayenne pepper

black and natural sesame seeds

Cape Charles House B&B
645 Tazwell Ave
Cape Charles, VA
757-331-4920
www.capecharleshouse.com
stay@capecharleshouse.com

A Continental Courtship

1868 CROSBY HOUSE

Citrus Croissants

INGREDIENTS:

6 large crescent croissants, split in half, lengthwise

4 eggs

1/2 cup milk (low-fat works fine)

1/2 cup chunky style orange marmalade

1/2 cup real maple syrup (we use Fancy grade)

1868 Crosby House
175 Western Avenue
Brattleboro, VT
802-257-7145
www.crosbyhouse.com
lynn@crosbyhouse.com

INSTRUCTIONS:
Combine 1/2 cup orange marmalade with 1/2 maple syrup. Heat in the microwave for 2 minutes on high. (This special syrup can be made ahead and refrigerated as it keeps well and gets better each day – be sure to heat it before drizzling on croissants)

Split croissants lengthwise and dip into egg/milk mixture. Let set insides up while you preheat your griddle to 350 degrees F, lightly swipe with butter and cook the croissants on both sides like French toast, but watch carefully – they brown and cook quickly because they are airy. (Do not flatten)

Serve in a spiral of 3 on a warmed plate with a meat of your choice. Drizzle lightly with hot orange syrup (recipe above). Just before serving, squirt a rosette of whipped cream on the top and dust cream rosette with nutmeg.

COOK TIME: *15 min*
YIELD: *4 servings*

Inn Love

AVENUE HOTEL BED AND BREAKFAST

Almond Poppy Seed Muffins

INSTRUCTIONS:

Beat together the eggs, white sugar and oil. Add milk, almond extract, vanilla extract. Sift in flour, salt and baking powder. Fold in poppy seeds.

Spray muffin tins with non-stick cooking spray. Fill muffin cups 2/3 full. Bake the muffins at 375 degrees F for 20 minutes.

For the glaze: In a saucepan over low heat, combine sugar, butter, orange juice, vanilla and almond extract; warm in pan until sugar is dissolved. Dunk the tops of the muffins into the glaze.

COOK TIME: *20 min*
YIELD: *2 dozen*

Avenue Hotel Bed and Breakfast
711 Manitou Ave
Manitou Springs, CO
719-685-1277
www.avenuehotelbandb.com
info@avenuehotelbandb.com

INGREDIENTS:

For the muffins:

3 eggs

2½ cup (less 2 tbsp) white sugar

1 cup vegetable oil

3½ cup flour

1½ cup milk

1½ tsp vanilla extract

2 tsp almond extract

1½ tsp salt

1¼ tsp baking powder

2 tbsp poppy seeds

For the glaze:

3/4 cup white sugar

1/4 cup orange juice

1/2 tsp vanilla extract

1/2 tsp almond extract

2 tsp butter

A Continental Courtship

TEFFT HOUSE BED AND BREAKFAST
Rhubarb-Pecan Muffins

INGREDIENTS:

2 cups flour

3/4 cup sugar

3/4 cup chopped pecans

1 ½ tsp baking powder

1 tsp salt

1/2 tsp baking soda

1 egg

2 tsp orange zest

3/4 cup orange juice

1/4 cup canola oil

1¼ cups finely chopped rhubarb

1/4 cup light brown sugar

INSTRUCTIONS:
Preheat the oven to 400 degrees F.

In a large bowl, combine flour, sugar, pecans, baking powder, salt, and baking soda. In another bowl, beat together the egg, orange zest, orange juice, and canola oil. Stir in the rhubarb. Make a well in the center of the flour mixture. Pour the rhubarb mixture in all at once. Stir until moistened (the batter should be lumpy). Spray muffin cups with baking spray. Fill each cup 2/3 full. Sprinkle the tops with the brown sugar.

Bake for 20 minutes or until golden. Remove from pans. Serve immediately.

COOK TIME: *20 min*
YIELD: *16 servings*

Tefft House Bed and Breakfast
20 W Broadway
Plainview, MN
507-534-3001
www.teffthouse.com
info@teffthouse.com

BLACK WALNUT GUEST HOUSE

Cranberry Orange Muffins

INGREDIENTS:

- 2 cups flour
- 1/2 cup sugar
- 2 tsp baking powder
- 1/2 tsp salt
- 2 eggs lightly beaten
- 1/2 cup orange juice
- 1/2 cup oil
- 1 cup chopped cranberries
- 2 tsp freshly grated orange peel
- 1/4 cup sugar
- *Optional:* 1/2 cup chopped nuts

INSTRUCTIONS:

Grease muffin tin. Combine dry ingredients. In a separate small bowl mix cranberries, orange peel and sugar, set aside. Mix liquid ingredients then add to combined dry ingredients and stir until just moistened. Fold in cranberry mix. Put into muffin tin.

Bake at 375 degrees F. Makes 6 jumbo baked for 25 minutes or 12 med baked 15–20 minutes.

COOK TIME: *15–25 min*
YIELD: *6 jumbo or 12 medium muffins*

Black Walnut Guest House
454 North 7th Ave
Sturgeon Bay, WI
920-743-8892
www.blackwalnut-gh.com
stay@blackwalnut-gh.com

Love is being stupid together.

PAUL VALERY

A Continental Courtship 23

INN AT ELLIS RIVER

Triple Chocolate Banana Muffins

INGREDIENTS:

4½ cups flour

2 tbsp baking powder

2 cups sugar

1/2 cup + 1 tbsp Dutch processed cocoa

1/2 tsp salt

3 medium bananas, mashed

2 eggs, slightly beaten

1/2 cup melted butter, cooled

1 tsp vanilla

1/2 cup sour cream or low fat yogurt

2 cups milk

3/4 cup premium quality white chocolate chips, such as Ghirardelli

3/4 cup premium quality double chocolate chips, such as Ghirardelli

Confectioner's sugar for dusting tops

INSTRUCTIONS:
Preheat oven to 400 degrees F. Whisk flour, baking powder, sugar, cocoa, and salt together.

Mix eggs, butter, sour cream and vanilla into mashed bananas. Gradually add milk to mixture. Add wet mixture to dry ingredients, and mix gently until almost combined. Fold in chocolate chips. Do not over mix.

Spray muffin tins with a non-stick spray, and fill about 2/3 full. Bake for 22–25 minutes, or until test utensil comes clean. Let cool slightly, remove from baking pan, and dust with confectioner's sugar before serving.

COOK TIME: *25 min*
YIELD: *2 dozen*

Inn at Ellis River
PO Box 656
Jackson, NH
603-383-9339
www.innatellisriver.com
stay@innatellisriver.com

FITCH HILL INN

Cranberry Crunch Muffins

Fitch Hill Inn
258 Fitch Hill Rd
Hyde Park, VT
802-888-3834
www.fitchhillinn.com
innkeeper@fitchhillinn.com

INSTRUCTIONS:

Mix cranberries with 1–2 tablespoons sugar and set aside. Combine flour, sugar, baking powder, salt and orange rind into a large bowl. Using a whisk, combine egg, cooking oil, milk, and orange juice in another bowl, mix well. Add egg mixture all at once to dry ingredients, stirring just until moistened. Small lumps are OK. Fold in cranberries. Spoon batter into greased regular sized muffin cups, filling 2/3 full.

For topping, place sugar, flour and butter in food processor. Process to the consistency of course corn meal. Add pecans and process to desired consistency. Sprinkle over muffins.

Bake at 350 degrees F for 30 minutes.

COOK TIME: *30 min*
YIELD: *1 dozen*

INGREDIENTS:

1 cup fresh or frozen cranberries, coarsely chopped

2 tbsp sugar

2 cups all-purpose flour

2 tbsp sugar

3 tsp baking powder

1/2 tsp salt

1/2 tsp grated orange rind

2 eggs, beaten

3/4 cup cooking oil

3/4 cup milk

1/4 cup orange juice

Streusel Topping:

1/8 cup sugar

1/8 cup flour

1/4 cup chopped pecans

1 tbsp butter

A Continental Courtship

POOLSIDE PARADISE B&B

Sour Cream Blueberry Muffins

INGREDIENTS:

1/4 cup butter, room temperature

3/4 cup sugar

2 eggs

1¼ cup plus 2 tbsp sifted flour

1/2 tsp baking soda

1/4 tsp salt

3/4 cup sour cream

1 cup blueberries

1/2 tsp vanilla

INSTRUCTIONS:

Preheat oven to 450 degrees F and line muffin tin with paper liners. In a medium bowl, cream butter, sugar, and vanilla. Add eggs one at a time, beating well after each. Sift flour, soda, and salt together, and add to butter mixture alternately with sour cream. Gently fold in berries. Bake for 12–15 minutes until golden brown. Makes 12 muffins. *(Recipe can be doubled, if desired.)*

NOTE: This recipe will also work in a pan for a coffee cake. If I put it into a pan, I usually just add a topping of chopped nuts (any kind) mixed with a little sugar (white or brown), cinnamon and nutmeg. Often I swirl the topping into the batter but leave most of the topping on the top of the cake.

COOK TIME: *15 min*
YIELD: *1 dozen*

Poolside Paradise B&B

Box 220
Clinton, BC
250-459-7990
www.poolsideparadisebb.com
poolsideparadisebb@bcwireless.com

Inn Love

A TREEHOUSE B&B

Sun-Dried Tomato and Feta Crown Muffins

INSTRUCTIONS:
Preheat oven to 400 degrees F.

Mix together flour, sugar, Italian seasonings, baking powder, salt and baking soda. Add combined milk, butter, egg, and tomatoes; mix just until dry ingredients are moistened. Gently fold in feta cheese.

Fill muffin pan cups about 3/4 full (about 1/4 cup batter). Bake 10–12 minutes or until wooden pick inserted in center comes out clean. Let muffin crowns stand a few minutes, remove from pan. Cool on wire rack.

NOTE: *Montrachet cheese can be substituted. We use EKKO Baker's Secret Muffins Crowns muffin pans.*

COOK TIME: *10–12 min*
YIELD: *6 servings*

INGREDIENTS:

1½ cups of all-purpose flour

2 tsp sugar

1½ tsp Italian herb seasonings

1 tsp baking powder

1/2 tsp salt

1/8 tsp baking soda

1/2 cup milk

1/4 cup butter, melted

1 egg, slightly beaten

8 sun-dried tomatoes, packed in oil, well-drained & chopped

2 ounces feta, chopped

A TreeHouse B&B
2490 W 49th Ave
Vancouver, BC
604-266-2962
www.treehousebb.com
bb@treehousebb.com

A Continental Courtship

THE HURST HOUSE

Baked Oatmeal

INGREDIENTS:

2 eggs

1/2 cup cooking oil

1 cup sugar

3 cup oatmeal

1 cup milk

2 tsp baking powder

1/4 tsp salt

Optional additions:

1/2 tsp cinnamon

1/2 cup raisins or chopped apples

INSTRUCTIONS:
Mix together the 3 first ingredients. Add remaining items. Pour into a 2-quart casserole or 9×9 inch pan. Bake for 30 minutes at 350 degrees F.

NOTES: *Can prepare the night before, cover and refrigerate. Remove from refrigerator 15 min. before placing in preheated oven.*

COOK TIME: *30 min*
YIELD: *6 servings*

Love is a smoke made with the fume of sighs.

WILLIAM SHAKESPEARE

The Hurst House
154 East Farmersville Road
Ephrata, PA
717-355-5151
www.hursthousebedandbreakfast.com
TheHurstHouse@gmail.com

Inn Love

FLOWERS AND THYME BED & BREAKFAST
Date Nut Bread

INGREDIENTS:

- 2 cups chopped dates
- 1½ cups boiling water
- 2 cups sugar
- 1 egg
- 1 tsp vanilla
- 1/2 tsp salt
- 1 cup butter
- 1 cup nuts
- 3 cups flour
- 1/2 tsp cinnamon
- 1/4 tsp nutmeg
- 2 tsp baking soda

INSTRUCTIONS:
Pour water over dates and let stand.

Cream together sugar, egg, vanilla, salt and butter; set aside.

Mix together nuts, flour, cinnamon, nutmeg and baking soda; then add to the creamed mixture and stir till blended. Add the date mixture.

Pour into a 13×9-inch pan. Bake at 350 degrees F for about 45 minutes.

COOK TIME: *45 minutes*

Flowers and Thyme Bed & Breakfast
238 Strasburg Pike
Lancaster, PA
717-393-1460
www.flowersandthyme.com
stay@flowersandthyme.com

A Continental Courtship

THE RICHMOND VICTORIAN INN

Blueberry Cream Cheese Casserole

The Richmond Victorian Inn
PO Box 652
Richmond, VT
802-434-4410
www.richmondvictorianinn.com
innkeeper@richmond-victorianinn.com

INGREDIENTS:

12 slices sourdough, white or wheat bread

2 (8 oz) packages cream cheese

1½ cups blueberries, fresh or frozen, divided

12 eggs

2 cups milk (skim, low fat or regular)

1/3 cup Vermont maple syrup

1 tsp ground cinnamon

INSTRUCTIONS:

Cut bread into bite-sized cubes. Place half in buttered 13×9-inch pan or casserole dish. Cut 1 package cream cheese into 1" cubes and place over bread. Top with 3/4 cup blueberries. Repeat process with remaining bread, cream cheese, and blueberries. In separate bowl beat eggs and add milk, maple syrup, and cinnamon. Mix well and pour over bread layers. Cover with foil and refrigerate 8 to 10 hours or overnight.

When ready to cook, remove casserole from refrigerator. Preheat oven to 350 degrees F and bake casserole, covered, 30 minutes. Uncover and bake 25 to 30 minutes more, or until knife inserted near center comes out clean. Serve warm with blueberry or Vermont maple syrup and bacon or sausage.

COOK TIME: *1 hour*
YIELD: *12 servings*

HOLLY COURT INN

Almond Raspberry Coffee Cake

INSTRUCTIONS:

Grease bottom and sides of a 9-inch spring form pan. Sprinkle bottom of pan with breadcrumbs.

Mix flour, sugar, and salt. Add butter and mix until mixture resembles coarse crumbs. (A food processor works well for this). Remove 1 cup of mixture to a separate bowl. Reserve for topping.

Mix in baking powder and soda. Add buttermilk or yogurt, egg, vanilla and almond extract. Mix until mixture is smooth and fluffy. Pour into prepared pan and smooth top. Mix raspberry jam until fluid and spread over batter.

Add ground almonds, sugar, egg yolk and almond extract to reserved crumb mixture from step #1. Mix well with fingers. Sprinkle topping evenly over cake batter.

Bake at 350 degrees F for 50 to 65 minutes (until toothpick inserted in center is clean). Cool in pan on rack for 10 minutes. Slide thin knife around sides of pan and remove. Cool on rack at least 1½ hours before serving.

COOK TIME: *55 min*

Holly Court Inn
301 S Alexander Ave
Washington, GA
706-678-3982
www.hollycourtinn.com
info@hollycourtinn.com

INGREDIENTS:

dry breadcrumbs

2 cups all-purpose flour

1⅛ cup sugar

1 tsp salt

1¼ cup (10 tablespoons) unsalted butter

1 tsp baking powder

1/2 tsp baking soda

3/4 cup buttermilk or yogurt

1 large egg

1 tsp vanilla

1 tsp almond extract

1/2 cup seedless raspberry jam

Topping:

3/4 cup ground almonds

1/2 cup sugar

1 large egg yolk

1 tsp almond extract

A Continental Courtship **31**

ALEGRIA OCEANFRONT INN & COTTAGES

Crumb Coffee Cake with Cream

INGREDIENTS:

Raspberry topping:

1 cup fresh or frozen raspberries
1/4 cup apple juice
3 tbsp sugar
1 tsp cornstarch
2 tsp water

Alegria Oceanfront Inn & Cottages
PO Box 803
Mendocino, CA
707-937-5150
www.oceanfrontmagic.com
inn@oceanfrontmagic.com

INSTRUCTIONS:

Butter and flour a 9- or 10-inch springform pan. Preheat oven to 350 degrees F.

For raspberry topping: Place raspberries and apple juice in a small saucepan. Bring to boil and then simmer for a few minutes. Add 3 tablespoon sugar (or to taste). Combine cornstarch & water. Add a small bit of warm raspberry juice to cornstarch mixture, then add mixture to raspberries. Continue to simmer until reduced to about 3/4 cup raspberry goop (won't take long).

For crumb mixture and batter: Pulse flour, 3/4 cup sugar & sweet butter in a food processor until the mixture resembles coarse crumbs.

Reserve 1 cup of mixture and set aside. Pour remaining into a large bowl and stir in baking powder, baking soda, salt & lemon zest. Whip together: 1 egg, yogurt (or buttermilk) & 1 teaspoon vanilla extract and add to large bowl. Stir together until just combined. Batter will be sticky. Spread evenly along bottom of pan then up the sides about 1/4 inch. Use a small offset stainless steel spatula.

For topping: Beat together or whirl in food processor until smooth: cream cheese, 1/4 cup sugar, 1 egg, and 1 teaspoon vanilla extract. Spread over the well of batter. Carefully spread and swirl raspberry goop over cream cheese mixture. It'll be uneven, but don't worry. Add sliced almonds to the crumb mixture in the small bowl and sprinkle evenly over raspberry goop and batter edge.

Bake at 350 degrees F for 35–45 minutes or until filling is set and cake is light golden brown. Cool 10 minutes before removing sides.

Cheese and Raspberry Topping

YIELD: *12 servings*
COOK TIME: *45 min*

For crumb mixture and batter:

2¼ cups flour

3/4 cup sugar

1/2 cup sweet butter cut into 1 tbsp slices

1/2 tsp baking powder

1/2 tsp baking soda

1/4 tsp salt

zest of a small lemon

1 egg

3/4 cup plain low-fat yogurt or buttermilk

1 tsp vanilla extract

Topping:

6 oz cream cheese, softened

1 egg

1/4 cup sugar

1 tsp vanilla extract

1/2 cup sliced almonds

A Continental Courtship

B&B AT ROSELEDGE HERB FARM

Cape Cod Cranberry Coffee Cake

INGREDIENTS:

For the cranberry filling:

1½ cups whole or chopped cranberries (I use whole)

1/4 cup water

2/3 cup sugar

2 tablespoons cornstarch

For the streusel topping:

1/4 cup sugar

1/4 cup all-purpose flour

1 tbsp flour

1 tbsp butter

1 tbsp sliced almonds (optional)

INSTRUCTIONS:

To prepare the cranberry filling:
In a small saucepan, combine the cranberries and water. Bring to a boil. Lower the heat and simmer, covered, for 5 minutes or until tender.

In a small bowl, stir together the 2/3 cup sugar and the cornstarch, then stir into cranberry mixture. Cook over moderate heat, stirring constantly, for 4 minutes or until mixture is thickened. Remove from heat.

Preheat oven to 350 degrees F.

To prepare streusel topping: In medium-size bowl, stir together the 1/4 cup sugar and the 1/4 cup flour. Using a pastry blender or 2 knives, cut in the 1 tablespoon butter until mixture resembles coarse crumbs. Stir in almonds (if using). Set aside.

To prepare the coffee cake: In a large bowl, stir together the 1 ½ cups flour, 1/2 cup sugar, baking powder, baking soda, and nutmeg.

Flowers are happy things.

P. G. WODEHOUSE

Using a pastry blender or 2 knives, cut in the 3 tablespoons butter until the mixture resembles coarse crumbs. In a small bowl, combine the egg whites, buttermilk, and vanilla. Add to flour mixture all at once and stir just until combined.

Spread two-thirds of the batter into a lightly greased 9-inch round pan *(I use a cheese cake pan so that I can display it better)*. Spread the cranberry filling over batter. Drop the remaining batter in small mounds on top of cranberry filling. Sprinkle with streusel topping. Bake 35 to 40 minutes or until golden. Serve warm.

COOK TIME: *35–40 min*
YIELD: *9 servings*

For the coffee cake:

1½ cups all-purpose flour

1/2 cup sugar

1/2 tsp baking powder

1/4 tsp baking soda

1/4 tsp ground nutmeg

3 tbsp butter

2 large egg whites

1/2 cup low-fat buttermilk or soured milk

1 tsp vanilla

B&B at Roseledge Herb Farm
418 route 164
Preston, CT
860-892-4739
www.roseledge.com
roseledgefarm@aol.com

A Continental Courtship

WAIANUHEA B&B

Zucchini Carrot Coconut Macadamia Nut Bread

INGREDIENTS:

1½ cup whole wheat flour

1½ cup white flour

1 tsp salt

1 tsp baking powder

1 tsp baking soda

3 tsp cinnamon

3 eggs

1 cup vegetable oil

2¼ cup sugar

3 tsp vanilla

1 cup grated carrot

1 cup grated zucchini

1 cup chopped Macadamia nuts

1 cup coconut

Waianuhea B&B
PO Box 185
Honokaa, HI
808-775-1118
www.waianuhea.com
info@waianuhea.com

INSTRUCTIONS:
Whisk flour, salt, soda, baking powder and cinnamon in small bowl. Whisk egg, oil, sugar and vanilla in large bowl. Fold dry ingredients into egg mixture then add carrot, zucchini, macadamia nuts and coconut. Separate batter evenly in two greased loaf pans, bake and cool at least 10 minutes before enjoying!

Created with Aloha in Ahualoa, Hawaii by Randy Goff.

COOK TIME: *1 hr*
YIELD: *2 loaves*

A kiss on the hand may be quite continental, but diamonds are a girl's best friend.

LEO ROBIN

Inn Love

THE SETTLERS INN AT BINGHAM PARK

Rhubarb Bread

INGREDIENTS:

3 cups packed brown sugar

1 cup corn oil

2 eggs

1½ tsp vanilla

1½ tsp baking soda

1½ tsp salt

4½ cups flour

2½ cups rhubarb

Springtime gives us this unusual bread that we find very appealing. With its tart sweet flavor, we like serving it with strawberry cream cheese.

INSTRUCTIONS:
Blend the oil and sugar. Add the eggs and vanilla mixing until creamy. Sift the dry ingredients and stir into the sugar mix until blended. Fold in the rhubarb and divide between 2 greased loaf pans. Bake (350 degrees F) for about 45 minutes to an hour, or until a tester comes out clean.

NOTE: *If using frozen rhubarb, thaw and increase flour to 5 cups. Use the rhubarb liquid.*

COOK TIME: *45 min*
YIELD: *2 loaves*

The Settlers Inn at Bingham Park
4 Main Ave
Hawley, PA
570-226-2993
www.thesettlersinn.com
jeanne@thesettlersinn.com

A Continental Courtship

HARBORSIDE HOUSE

Orange Muffin Bread

INGREDIENTS:

3 cups flour

4 tsp baking powder

3/4 cup sugar

1/4 tsp salt

1 egg

1¼ cups orange juice

2/3 cup oil (canola or safflower)

3/4 cup toasted wheat germ

3/4 cup chopped nuts

3/4 cup dried cranberries

2 tsp grated orange peel (optional)

Harborside House
23 Gregory St
Marblehead, MA
781-631-1032
www.harborsidehouse.com
stay@harborsidehouse.com

INSTRUCTIONS:

Sift together flour, baking powder, sugar, and salt. Combine egg, orange juice, orange peel, and oil. Add liquid ingredients to dry and mix gently. Fold in nuts, wheat germ, and dried cranberries.

For bread:
Pour into greased pan. Bake at 350 degrees F for 50–55 minutes. Cool in pan 10 minutes then remove onto wire rack.

For muffins:
Line muffin cups or grease well. Bake at 400 degrees F for 15 minutes.

COOK TIME: *10–15 min*
YIELD: *2 loaves*

ALBERT SHAFSKY HOUSE B&B

Banana Cranberry Nut Bread

INSTRUCTIONS:
Mix ingredients in order listed. Pour into a greased loaf pan or muffin pan. Bake 1 hour at 350 degree F. Test for doneness, as it may need an additional 5 to 15 minutes baking time.

COOK TIME: *about 1 hour*
YIELD: *1 loaf*

INGREDIENTS:
- 1/2 cup butter
- 1 cup sugar
- 2 eggs
- 3 bananas, mashed
- 2 cups flour
- 1 tsp baking soda
- 1/4 cup nutmeats
- 1/2 cup dried cranberries

I like perfume and flowers.

DONATELLA VERSACE

Albert Shafsky House B&B
2942 Coloma St
Placerville, CA
530-642-2776
www.shafsky.com
stay@shafsky.com

A Continental Courtship

WARE STREET INN

Tropical Blend Banana Bread

INGREDIENTS:

2 cups all-purpose flour

1½ tsp baking powder

1/2 tsp baking soda

1/2 tsp salt

2 eggs, slightly beaten

1 cup sugar

1 cup mashed ripe bananas (3 medium)

1/2 cup strawberry-banana or vanilla yogurt

1½ tsp vanilla

1/2 cup chopped walnuts, pecans or macadamia nuts

1/2 cup flaked coconut

INSTRUCTIONS:

Grease bottom and 1/2 inch up sides of 9×5×3-inch pan or two 7 ½ × 3½ × 2-inch pans; set aside. In a large mixing bowl, combine flour, baking powder, baking soda and sale. Make a well in center of mixture, set aside.

In a separate mixing bowl combine eggs, sugar, bananas, butter, yogurt and vanilla. Add egg mixture all at once to flour mixture. Stir till just moistened (batter should be lumpy). Fold in nuts and coconut. Spoon batter into prepared pan(s).

Bake the banana bread in a 350 degree oven F for 1 to 1 ¼ hours for one large pan and for 40–45 minutes for two smaller pans, or till wooden toothpick inserted near center comes out clean (if necessary, cover loosely with foil the last 15 to 20 minutes of baking to prevent over-browning).

Cool in pan on a wire rack for 10 minutes. Remove from pan. Cool completely on a wire rack. Wrap and store overnight before serving.

COOK TIME: *1–1 ¼ hrs*
YIELD: *1–2 loaves*

Ware Street Inn
52 Ware St
Lewiston, ME
207-783-8171
www.warestreetinn.com
info@warestreetinn.com

NORTH LODGE ON OAKLAND

Raspberry-Cheese Coffee Cake

North Lodge on Oakland
84 Oakland Rd
Asheville, NC
828-252-6433
www.northlodge.com
stay@northlodge.com

NOTE: *You will need 3 bowls*

INSTRUCTIONS:
Heat oven to 325 degrees F.

Butter and flour a 10-inch spring form pan.

Combine first set of ingredients in a small bowl and set aside. Combine second set of ingredients in a small bowl and set aside. Combine third set of ingredients in large bowl, then cut in butter. Remove 1 cup of flour mixture from combined dry ingredients (with butter).

Add sour cream mixture to remaining flour mixture, stirring just until dry ingredients are moistened. Spread batter with spatula into prepared pan and spread evenly over bottom and 2 inches up the sides of the pan. Spread cream cheese mixture evenly over batter.

Drizzle raspberry preserves over cream cheese mixture. Sprinkle with reserved 1 cup of flour mixture. Sprinkle almonds over flour mixture. Bake 1 hour. Cool 15 minutes.

COOK TIME: *1 hr*

INGREDIENTS:
In a little bowl:

1 (8 oz) package cream cheese, softened 1 minute in the microwave

1/2 cup sugar

1 egg, beaten

In a little bowl:

1 cup sour cream

1 tsp almond flavor

1 egg, beaten

In a large bowl:

2½ cup flour

1 tsp baking powder

1 tsp baking soda

3/4 cup sugar

3/4 cup butter

Also have on hand:

3/4 cup raspberry preserves (or any other flavor you want)

3/4 cup sliced almonds

A Continental Courtship

An Eggs-Travagant Affair

EXTREMELY VERSATILE and excellently healthy, the egg makes for a delicious meal any time of day. Hard boiled, poached, or sunny side up, they shift and shape into everyone's breakfast favorite. Folded, stirred, or crisped, they add the fluff, puff, and crust to mouthwatering morning meals. Wake up early and watch the sun bathe your kitchen, while you and your honey recreate one of these bed and breakfast gems. Whatever time you choose to bring these classic bed and breakfast recipes to life, you and your loved one will surely enjoy an eggs-quisite meal.

> *A kiss is a lovely trick designed by nature to stop speech when words become superfluous.*
>
> INGRID BERGMAN

An Eggs-Travagant Affair

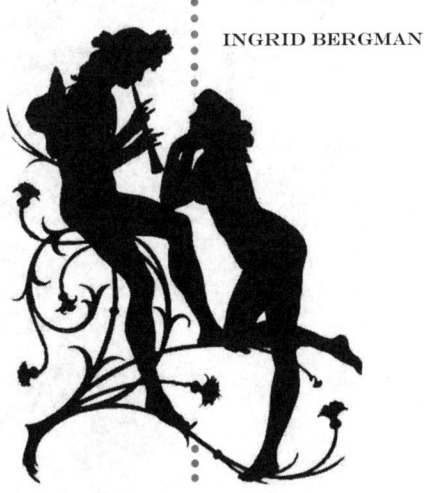

TIMMERMANN HOUSE B&B

Baked Eggs Florentine

INGREDIENTS:

- 6 oz creamed spinach
- 2 tbsp chopped red pepper (sautéed)
- 4 slices ham
- 1/2 cup chopped water chestnuts
- 4 eggs
- 1/8 tsp ground nutmeg
- salt & pepper
- 1/2 cup shredded Monterrey Jack

This recipe is dedicated to my dear friend Sue who loved life, appreciated good food (including this recipe) and wine.

INSTRUCTIONS:

Preheat oven to 400 degrees F. Microwave spinach on high 5–6 min. Grease 4 baking dishes, and place a piece of ham in each. Divide spinach in each dish making an indentation. Sprinkle water chestnuts and carefully break egg in each dish. Season with nutmeg, salt & pepper. Bake 15–20 minutes until egg is set, sprinkle cheese and red peppers, and then bake until cheese is melted.

COOK TIME: *30 min*
YIELD: *4 servings*

Timmermann House B&B
6130 Old US Hwy 50
Aviston, IL
618-228-7068
timmermannhouse.com
timmermannhouse@sbcglobal.net

Inn Love

BUTTONWOOD INN

The Innkeeper's Souffle

INSTRUCTIONS:
Beat egg yolks, add sour cream, water, Tabasco, herbs, salt and pepper and mix well. Beat whites till soft peaks form, fold gently into yolk mixture. Then fold in cheese. Pour into two 6 oz. custard cups. Bake 12–14 minutes in 350 degree F oven.

COOK TIME: *15 min*
YIELD: *2 servings*

For it was not into my ear you whispered, but into my heart. It was not my lips you kissed, but my soul.

JUDY GARLAND

INGREDIENTS:

2 eggs, separated with the whites at room temperature

1 heaping tbsp sour cream (plain yogurt or cottage cheese in a pinch!)

1 tbsp cold water

4 or 5 drops Tabasco Sauce

1 tsp dried mixed herbs or 2 tbsp fresh

mixed herbs, parsley, basil, rosemary, chives, oregano, or thyme.

salt and pepper to taste

1/4 cup shredded cheddar cheese

Buttonwood Inn
50 Admiral Dr
Franklin, NC
828-369-8985
www.buttonwoodbb.com
lizp1939@frontier.com

An Eggs-Travagant Affair

ELLERY HOUSE
Featherbed Eggs

INGREDIENTS:

2 slices country French bread, 3/4 inch thick

1 cup aged extra sharp cheddar cheese, grated

1/4 cup diced ham

3 large eggs

1/2 cup half-and-half

freshly ground pepper to taste

INSTRUCTIONS:

Place bread slice on bottom of buttered 1-quart glass casserole dish. Tuck in bread pieces to fill any gaps. Cover with grated cheese. Sprinkle with ham. Mix eggs and enough half-and-half together to make about 1 cup of liquid. Drizzle egg/half-and-half mixture over top of cheese and ham. Grind black pepper over the top. Cover and refrigerate overnight or at least 6 hours. Put in cold oven and turn oven to 350 degrees F. Bake, uncovered, for about 45 minutes until puffy and lightly golden.

COOK TIME: *45 minutes*
YIELD: *2 servings*

Ellery House
28 S 21st Ave E
Duluth, MN
218-724-7639
www.elleryhouse.com
info@elleryhouse.com

A kiss makes the heart young again and wipes out the years.

RUPERT BROOKE

THE WINE COUNTRY INN & GARDENS
Sourdough Eggs

INGREDIENTS:

12 slices of toasted and lightly buttered extra-sourdough bread

4 cups grated sharp cheddar cheese

1/2 medium onion, diced

1 cup thinly sliced mushrooms

10 eggs

4 cups milk

3 heaping tbsp of spicy mustard

1 tsp salt

1/4 tsp pepper

INSTRUCTIONS:
Cut bread into small cubes. Place 1/2 of bread cubes into large coated baking dish. Sprinkle with 2 cups cheese, onion, and mushrooms. Add second layer of bread and top with remaining cheese.

Beat eggs, milk, mustard, salt and pepper together. Pour this mixture evenly over the casserole. Cover with foil and refrigerate overnight. Bake at 325 degrees F for approximately 50 minutes until top is golden and lightly crusted.

YIELD: *6 servings*

The Wine Country Inn & Gardens
1152 Lodi Ln
St. Helena, CA
707-963-7077
www.winecountryinn.com
jim@winecountryinn.com

An Eggs-Travagant Affair

CRIMSON COTTAGE INN THE WOODS

Italian Sausage and Egg Casserole

INGREDIENTS:

6 slices bread, crusts removed

1½ or 2 cups shredded mozzarella cheese, or/and Italian mix of shredded cheese

1/4 cup of feta cheese

6 eggs, beaten well

2 cups half & half

sun-dried tomatoes (about 6 slices from a package)

2 lbs Italian sausage

1 tsp salt

Crimson Cottage Inn the Woods

2009 W. Lakewood Blvd.
Holland, MI
616-994-0922
www.crimsoncottageinn.com
kathy@crimsoncottageinn.com

INSTRUCTIONS:

Spray a 9×13-inch casserole with Pam or other non stick spray.

Cook sausage until well done, no longer pink. Drain. Tear bread into pieces and sprinkle in casserole pan. Sprinkle cooked sausage over bread. Sprinkle shredded cheese over sausage. Beat eggs with half & half and salt. Pour over mixture in casserole. Cut sun-dried tomatoes into small pieces and sprinkle over mixture. Sprinkle feta cheese over mixture. Cover and chill at least 8 hours or overnight. Bake at 350 degrees F for 45–50 minutes *(May need to cover last 10 minutes to prevent over-browning).*

COOK TIME: *50 min*
YIELD: *8 servings*

SIMPLY BED AND BREAD
Sunrise Service Egg Dish

INSTRUCTIONS:
Grease a 13×9×2 inch pan. Mix ingredients together. Bake at 350 degrees F for 40 minutes, or until done.

COOK TIME: *40 min*
YIELD: *8 servings*

INGREDIENTS:

1 cup Bisquick (I often make homemade, keep in freezer, then just use it, 1 cup at a time)

1 cup milk

6 eggs, slightly beaten

1 lb shredded pepper jack cheese

12 oz cottage cheese

1 stick melted butter

Simply Bed and Bread
208 Mt. Vernon Ave.
Chestertown, MD
410-778-4359
www.simplybedandbread.com
simplybedandbread@gmail.com

An Eggs-Travagant Affair

CARTER HOUSE INNS & RESTAURANT 301

Eggs Florentine *with Asiago Cheese*

INGREDIENTS:

Eggs Florentine:

- 6 eggs, perfectly poached
- 3 English muffins
- 1/4 cup butter
- 2 bunches fresh spinach
- 1/2 tsp nutmeg
- salt and white pepper to taste

Asiago Cheese Sauce:

- 2 scallions, finely chopped (white parts only)
- 1/2 cup white wine
- 4 cloves garlic, finely minced
- 1/2 cup Asiago cheese
- 1 cup heavy cream

INSTRUCTIONS:

In a saucepan, combine garlic, scallions, and wine. Reduce sauce over medium-high heat until wine is almost gone. Add the cream and reduce again until the mixture thickens noticeably. Add the asiago cheese and combine well. Keep sauce in a warm place until needed.

Slice and toast muffins and spread with butter.

Wilt spinach in a frying pan with fresh butter. Add salt and pepper to taste and sprinkle with approximately 1/4 teaspoon of nutmeg. Place spinach atop the buttered muffins. Lay poached eggs on top of the spinach. Cover with the cream sauce. Sprinkle with salt, pepper, and nutmeg before serving.

YIELD: *3 servings*

Carter House Inns & Restaurant 301
301 L St
Eureka, CA
707-444-8062
www.carterhouse.com
reserve@carterhouse.com

Inn Love

INN AT BATH

Green Chile Cheese Puff

INGREDIENTS:

- 1/4 cup all-purpose flour or cornmeal
- 3/4 tsp salt
- 1/2 tsp baking powder
- 6 large eggs
- 1 cup cottage cheese
- 1/2 lb grated cheddar cheese, (about 2 cups total)
- 3 small cans of chopped green chilies

INSTRUCTIONS:

Preheat the oven to 350 degrees F (Convection at 325 degrees). Place a rack at the middle level. Oil a 9-inch pie plate.

In a small bowl, sift together flour (or cornmeal), salt, and baking powder. In a large bowl, beat the eggs with an electric mixer until doubled in volume, about 3 minutes. Add the flour mixture and cheeses, and beat well. Stir in the chilies. Pour the mixture into the pie plate. Bake until the top is puffed and golden brown, and tester is just clean (still a bit moist is better than dry), 25–30 minutes.

Serve the egg puff immediately—it will fall slightly—with salsa on the side. This is great served with a fresh salsa, either tomato or mango. The cornmeal adds a bit of body, and is perfect when you have gluten-free/wheat-free guests.

NOTES: *I like cooking this in a smaller, deeper dish and scooping it instead. It is moister, a spoonful makes for a fun presentation, and people who don't "do quiche" won't dismiss it on principle.*

COOK TIME: *30 min*
YIELD: *6 servings*

Inn at Bath
969 Washington St
Bath, ME
207-443-4294
www.innatbath.com
innkeeper@innatbath.com

An Eggs-Travagant Affair

ARROYO VISTA INN'S
Eggs Florentine

INGREDIENTS:

3 tbsp pesto

1 cup Parmesan cheese, grated (divided)

1 cup mushrooms, sliced

1/2 cup tomatoes, sliced

3 cloves garlic, minced

2½ cups cottage cheese

2½ cups fresh spinach

1 cup mozzarella, grated

3–4 tbsp flour

2 cups milk

7 eggs

INSTRUCTIONS:

Grease 9×11-inch pan. Spread pesto and 1/2 cup grated Parmesan cheese over bottom of pan.

Sauté mushrooms, tomatoes and garlic together. When finished sautéing, mix with cottage cheese and spinach. Then put in pan over pesto.

In a separate bowl, mix together mozzarella, Parmesan cheese, flour milk and eggs. Pour mixture in the pan.

Bake 50–60 minutes at 350 degrees F.

COOK TIME: *50 min*
YIELD: *8 servings*

Arroyo Vista Inn
335 Monterey Rd
South Pasadena, CA
323-478-7300
www.arroyovistainn.com
info@arroyovistainn.com

MILL STREET INN

Grits Soufflé

INSTRUCTIONS:
Preheat oven to 375 degrees F.

In medium saucepan, scald two cups milk. Slowly add 1/2 cup grits, and stir over low heat until thickened. Add butter, salt, sugar, baking powder and dash of hot sauce. Remove from heat and mix well. Add beaten egg yolks, followed by egg whites beaten until stiff. Pour into greased quart casserole and bake in 375 degree F oven 25–29 minutes until puffed and golden. Serve immediately.

COOK TIME: *30 min*
YIELD: *6 servings*

INGREDIENTS:

2 cups milk

1/2 cup quick cooking hominy grits

2 tbsp butter

1 tsp salt

1/2 tsp sugar

1/2 tsp baking powder

3 eggs (separated)

dash Tabasco or other hot sauce

Mill Street Inn
114 Mill St
Cambridge, MD
410-901-9144
www.millstinn.com
jennie@millstinn.com

Life without love is like a tree without blossoms or fruit.

KHALIL GIBRAN

An Eggs-Travagant Affair

EARLYSTOWN MANOR

Spinach Omelet Roll

INGREDIENTS:

1 tbsp butter

1/2 red pepper, diced

3 green onions, sliced

1/2 cup crushed nacho chips

1/2 cup pico de gallo (preferably fresh)

1/2 cup sharp cheddar cheese, shredded

5 eggs

1 tsp cilantro

1/2 tsp fajita seasoning

1 tbsp water

Love is a game that two can play and both win.

EVA GABOR

INSTRUCTIONS:

Melt butter in 6 inch oven proof frying pan. Add pepper & onions saute till soft. Add crushed nacho chips, stir to coat. Remove pan from heat and evenly spread pico over pan mixture, then evenly spread cheese over pan mixture. Whisk together: eggs, cilantro, seasoning and water; and pour over pan mixture. Bake in 350 degrees F oven for 20 minutes or until puffed and golden. Let sit for 3 minutes, slice in 4 and serve with flour tortillas and fresh pico de gallo.

YIELD: *4 servings*

Earlystown Manor
400 Mill Race Ln
Wimberley, TX
512-847-9344
www.creekhaveninn.com
pat@creekhaveninn.com

Inn Love

DESERT DOVE B&B

Southwestern Frittata

INSTRUCTIONS:

The frittata should be prepared the day before and allowed to "cure" in the refrigerator overnight.

Brown sausage meat and drain off any excess fat, add pressed garlic to meat and cook for a few more minutes. Grease a 9×13-inch baking dish and evenly line the bottom of the dish with half of the chopped chilies, half of the tortilla strips, half of the sausage and half of the cheese. Repeat the layering with the other half of the chilies, tortilla strips, sausage and cheese. In a medium bowl, whisk the eggs, milk, salt, pepper, onion salt, and cumin until they are well mixed. Pour the mixture over the top of the dish. Sprinkle with chili powder to taste. Place thin slices of tomato over the top. Cover with plastic wrap and place in the refrigerator overnight to cure.

The next day, preheat the oven to 375 degrees F, remove the plastic wrap from the dish and bake the frittata for 45–50 minutes, or until the top is golden and the sides are a rich brown color. Cut into equal pieces and serve with a dollop of sour cream and salsa.

NOTES: *Serve with warm flour tortillas or your favorite toast! For vegetarians leave out the meat*

COOK TIME: *50 min*
YIELD: *8 servings*

Desert Dove B&B
11707 E Old Spanish Trl
Tucson, AZ
520-722-6879
www.desertdovebb.com
info@desertdovebb.com

INGREDIENTS:

1 (or more) cans of chopped mild green chilies

1 lb bulk sausage, cooked (ground turkey or chicken can be used in place of pork)

7 large eggs

1 large clove garlic (pressed)

1 tsp ground cumin

2 large ripe tomatoes (for slicing on top)

8 corn tortillas, sliced into small strips

1½ cups jack, cheddar or your favorite cheese, shredded

1 cup milk

1 tsp salt

1/2 tsp onion salt

1/4 tsp black pepper

chili powder to your taste

light sour cream

An Eggs-Travagant Affair

GRADY HOUSE HISTORIC BED & BREAKFAST

Vegetable Frittata/Strata

INGREDIENTS:

4 garlic cloves, minced

1 cup diced bread

4 tbsp extra virgin olive oil

1 cup chopped red onion

1/2 cup chopped red pepper

1/2 cup chopped yellow pepper

1/2 cup chopped green pepper

1 small crookneck squash, chopped

1/2 lb fresh spinach

1/2 lb baby bella mushrooms

Grady House Historic Bed & Breakfast

420 NW 1st Ave

High Springs, FL

386-454-2206

gradyhouse.com

lucie@gradyhouse.com

INSTRUCTIONS:

Preheat the oven to 350 degrees F. In a baking dish, toss together 2 of the minced garlic cloves, 2 tablespoons of olive oil and the bread cubes. Bake in the oven, stirring once, for 8 to 10 minutes, or until lightly toasted. Set aside.

In a skillet over medium heat, add 1 tablespoon of olive oil and the onion, peppers and squash. Sauté the vegetables for 6 to 7 minutes. Season with salt and pepper. Set aside.

In the same skillet, sauté two garlic cloves in 1 tablespoon of oil. Add mushrooms and sauté for 6 to 7 minutes until softened. Season with salt and pepper.

Place bread cubes into a lightly oiled 9×13-inch baking dish. Pour vegetable mixture on top. Place spinach leaves over top of vegetable layer. Pour mushrooms over top of spinach leaves. Spread cheeses on top of vegetables.

Inn Love

In a large bowl, whisk together eggs and milk. Pour egg mixture over cheese layer. Place halved grape tomatoes on top. Cover with foil and refrigerate overnight.

Remove from fridge and let stand 30 minutes before baking. Bake at 350 degrees F until set, about 40 to 50 minutes. Let stand for 10 minutes before cutting into squares to serve.

- 8 large eggs
- 2 cups half & half or whole milk
- 2 cups grated mozzarella cheese
- 1/4 cup grated Parmesan
- 1/4 cup grated Romano
- salt and pepper
- 1 tsp dried oregano
- 1/2 pint grape tomatoes, cut in half

At the touch of love everyone becomes a poet.

PLATO

An Eggs-Travagant Affair

THE SUMMER INN B&B
Smoked Salmon Strata

INGREDIENTS:

1½ cups bread pieces

1 cup chopped smoked salmon

2 cups shredded cheddar cheese

2 cups milk

6 eggs

1/4 tsp dry mustard

1/4 tsp cayenne pepper

1/4 tsp paprika

1/4 tsp pepper

parsley

Love is composed of a single soul inhabiting two bodies.

VIRGIL

INSTRUCTIONS:
Arrange the bread pieces in the bottom of a greased 9-inch square pan. Layer smoked salmon and Cheddar cheese over the bread. Cover with plastic wrap and refrigerate overnight. In a medium bowl beat the milk, eggs and spices. Pour over the refrigerated layers. Top with parsley. Bake in a 375 degree F oven for 40 to 45 minutes.

YIELD: *6 servings*

The Summer Inn B&B
PO Box 1198
Haines, AK
907-766-2970
www.summerinnbnb.com
innkeeper@summerinnbnb.com

VICTORIAN HOUSE B&B
Spinach-Sausage Quiche

INSTRUCTIONS:
Preheat oven to 375 degrees F.

In a medium skillet, cook sausage, onion and garlic over medium-high heat until the sausage is done, stirring occasionally. Drain mixture. Stir in spinach and stuffing mix.

Sprinkle first cheese and then sausage mixture in the pastry shell.

In a medium bowl, combine eggs and half & half with a fork or whisk until mixed well but not frothy. Pour egg mixture over sausage mixture in the pastry shell.

Bake 30 minutes. Sprinkle with Parmesan cheese and paprika. Bake 15 minutes or until knife inserted off-center comes out clean. Let stand 10 minutes before serving.

YIELD: *8 servings*

Victorian House B&B
11 Cadiz St
St. Augustine, FL
904-824-5214
www.victorianhousebnb.com
victorianhouse@bellsouth.net

INGREDIENTS:

1 refrigerated pastry shell

8 oz bulk pork sausage

1/4 cup red onion, chopped

1 garlic clove, minced

1/2 pkg (10oz pkg) frozen chopped spinach, cooked, drained well

1/2 cup herb-seasoned stuffing mix

1½ cup shredded Monterrey Jack cheese

3 eggs, slightly beaten

1½ cups half & half

2 tbsp grated Parmesan cheese

paprika

An Eggs-Travagant Affair

BRAZOS OAKS B&B

Smokey Cheddar and Bacon Quiche

INGREDIENTS:

1 unbaked pie shell

2 cup smoked cheddar

2 tbsp flour

4 eggs, beaten

1½ cup half & half

1 tsp salt

1/2 tsp black pepper

8 slices bacon, fried and cut into thin strips

INSTRUCTIONS:
Toss the cheese, flour and bacon together and spread evenly in the pie shell. Beat the eggs, half and half and seasonings together and pour over the cheese mixture.

Bake at 350 degrees F for 45 minutes or until set. Let sit for 5 minutes before serving.

NOTE: *I often half this recipe and make a small quiche for two in a 5 inch pie pan or 1/4 the recipe and make single quiches in mini pie pans.*

COOK TIME: *45 min*
YIELD: *6 servings*

Love is love's reward.

JOHN DRYDEN

Brazos Oaks B&B
6408 Gholson Rd
Waco, TX
254-744-7706
www.brazosbb.com
info@brazosbb.com

Inn Love

TEN BITS RANCH
Jen's Basic Quiche

INGREDIENTS:

1 (9-inch) pie shell

1½ cup heavy whipping cream

3 eggs

any precooked meat (like ground sausage or cubed ham)

shredded cheddar cheese

salt and pepper

Ten Bits Ranch
PO Box 293
Terlingua, TX
432-371-3110
www.tenbitsranch.com
tenbitsranch@BigBend.net

INSTRUCTIONS:
Preheat oven to 425 degrees F, put pie shell in a pan if it does not come in one and put pan on a cookie sheet, add meat and cheese to the pie shell. Then whisk the egg, cream, salt and pepper together. Now pour cream mixture over the meat and cheese then put in oven for 15 minutes. Next turn down oven to 300 degrees F and bake another 30 minutes or until done.

COOK TIME: *45 min*

An Eggs-Travagant Affair

HOLLAND INN

Avocado Quiche

INGREDIENTS:

1 cup sour cream

4 eggs, beaten

3 cups shredded cheddar cheese

dash of salt & black pepper to taste

8 scallions, chopped

2 ripe medium tomatoes, chopped then drained

2 ripe avocado, sliced about 1/4" thick

2 deep pie shells

Optional:
1/2 bunch fresh cilantro, chopped

INSTRUCTIONS:
Preheat oven to 375 degrees F.

Combine sour cream, eggs, salt and pepper. Mix well. Add cheese, mix well. Stir in scallions and tomatoes. Toss with cilantro (if used).

Lay avocado slices on the bottom of pie shells. There should be just enough slices to cover the bottom. Pour cheese mixture over avocado slices and spread out evenly.

Bake 40–45 minutes, until set and golden and puffy. Let stand 10 minutes before serving.

Top with a spoonful of sour cream and fresh chopped avocado, scallion and tomatoes.

COOK TIME: *45 min*
YIELD: *14 servings*

Holland Inn
35 Holland Ave

Bar Harbor, ME

207-288-4804

www.hollandinn.com

info@hollandinn.com

Do all things with love.

OG MANDINO

Inn Love

THE GRANGE AT STAG HOLLOW'S
Wine Country Quiche

INGREDIENTS:

For custard:

4 large eggs

1½ cups milk

pinch salt and pepper

1 (9-inch) frozen pie shell, thawed and pre-baked

6 pieces crisply cooked bacon, crumbled

2 green onions or scallions, washed and sliced

4 ounces coarsely grated Gruyere or Ementhaller cheese

The Grange at Stag Hollow

50 Firelane 11A RR3
Niagara on the Lake, ON
905-938-0698
www.staghollow.ca
thegrange@staghollow.ca

INSTRUCTIONS:

For custard: Whisk together in a bowl: 4 large eggs at room temperature, 12 ounces (1½ cups) whole milk or 2% milk at room temperature, and a pinch of salt and pepper.

Carefully pour the custard into the pre-baked pie shell allowing it to mix with the cheese, onion and bacon. Sprinkle on top 1/4 tsp. grated nutmeg (optional).

Return the quiche to the 400 degrees F oven and bake for 25 to 30 minutes or until the custard is set or a deep golden brown. Let sit a few minutes before cutting. Serve immediately.

COOK TIME: *30 min*
YIELD: *6 servings*

An Eggs-Travagant Affair

FAIRLEA FARM BED AND BREAKFAST

Quiche Havarti

INGREDIENTS:

1 sheet frozen puff pastry, thawed

3/4 cup all-purpose flour

1/2 tsp vanilla

3/4 cup milk

3 eggs

2 tablespoons butter, melted

pinch of salt

5 slices Havarti cheese, cut into small pieces

1 pear, unpeeled, cored and sliced thinly

Fairlea Farm Bed and Breakfast
PO Box 124
Washington, VA
540-675-3679
www.fairleafarm.com
longyear@shentel.net

INSTRUCTIONS:

Preheat oven to 400 degrees F. Grease 9×13-inch baking pan. Press puff pastry onto bottom of pan. Bake about 8 minutes until golden and puffed.

Mix together in medium-sized bowl flour, vanilla, milk, eggs, salt and melted butter. Beat until smooth.

Cool baked pastry a bit, and then top it with the sliced pear. Pour dough batter on top. Sprinkle cheese squares on top of batter, pressing some down into batter.

Bake about 20 to 30 minutes until edges are brown. Sprinkle with powdered sugar before serving.

Offer fresh preserves or jam to be eaten with quiche. Cut into squares and serve.

COOK TIME: *25 min*
YIELD: *8 servings*

BIG BEAR BED & BREAKFAST
Crustless Salmon Quiche

INSTRUCTIONS:

Bake At: 350 degrees F in boiling water (a small loaf pan holds 2 ramekins, an 8-inch square holds 4 ramekins, and a 9×13-inch holds 8 ramekins).

Pour blended mixture over & gently combine. Spray ramekins or quiche dish with non-stick spray. Can be made night before and refrigerated. Preheat filled ramekins in microwave on medium setting for 2–3 minutes prior to setting in boiling water. Bake in pan of boiling water for 30–45 minutes, bake as many portions as needed to serve. Refrigerate or freeze covered and uncooked portions. If frozen, thaw in refrigerator. Bake low in the oven to prevent a tough crust from developing on top.

Bake 30 minutes for small ramekins, and 45–60 minutes for a quiche or pie dish.

YIELD: *10 ramekins or 1 large quiche dish*

Big Bear Bed & Breakfast
3401 Richmond Ave
Anchorage, AK
907-277-8189
www.alaskabigbearbb.com
bigbearbb@alaska.net

INGREDIENTS:

Place in blender; blend till smooth:

4 eggs

1 cup sour cream

1 cup cottage cheese

1/4 cup flour

1/3 cup grated Parmesan cheese

1 tsp onion powder or granulated onion

1/4 tsp lemon pepper

Place in large bowl and mix together:

2 cups flaked red salmon (1 pint or lg. can, drained, baked or poached with skin and large bones removed)

1 (4-oz) can sliced or stems & pieces mushrooms, drained

4 oz grated Cheddar cheese

4 oz grated Monterrey jack cheese

1/2 tsp dill weed

An Eggs-Travagant Affair

FAIRVILLE INN

Spinach and Mushroom Quiche

INGREDIENTS:

1 lb mushrooms (white or crimini), diced.

2 tbsp olive oil, plus extra for coating the pan

salt

1 lb fresh spinach (or 1 (10 oz) package frozen chopped spinach, thawed and squeezed to remove excess water)

4 extra large eggs

1 cup ricotta cheese

1/2 cup crumbled feta cheese

INSTRUCTIONS:

Preheat the oven to 350 degrees F.

Sauté the diced mushrooms in the olive oil over medium high heat for 3 minutes, stirring occasionally. Sprinkle with salt to taste, lower the heat to medium and continue to sauté for an additional 4 minutes, stirring occasionally. You should have about 1 cup cooked mushrooms. Set aside.

If using fresh spinach, remove any coarse stems and microwave for 1 minute or until just wilted. Let cool a few minutes and then squeeze out excess water. Chop coarsely and set aside.

Using an electric mixer beat the eggs with the ricotta and feta cheeses until well blended. Beat in the seasonings. Stir in the mushrooms, spinach, parsley, and the green onions (if using).

Lightly grease the sauté pan with olive oil. Pour the quiche mixture into the pan and bake in the middle of the oven for about 45 minutes. The quiche is done when the center jiggles only slightly. Cool the pan on a wire rack for 15–20 minutes.

Fairville Inn

506 Kennett Pike, Rt 52

Chadds Ford, PA

610-388-5900

www.fairvilleinn.com

info@fairvilleinn.com

To serve, place a large flat pot cover over the pan and invert the quiche onto the cover. Place a serving plate over the bottom of the inverted quiche and flip over. With a serrated knife, cut the quiche into pie-like wedges.

COOK TIME: *45 min*
YIELD: *8 servings*

> ***Don't let love interfere with your appetite. It never does with mine.***
>
> ANTHONY TROLLOPE

1/4 tsp garlic powder (or more to taste)

1/2 tsp onion powder (or more to taste)

1/2 tsp freshly ground black or white pepper (or more to taste)

1/4 tsp ground nutmeg (optional)

3–4 green onions (white and light green parts), thinly sliced (optional)

2 tbsp finely chopped fresh parsley (Italian flat recommended)

Sweetheart Sunrise

PANCAKES, WAFFLES, CREPES, FRENCH TOAST — tempting and sweet, just like that special someone who lights up your life. Recreate these tried and true classics, and start your day with that touch of sweetness from your favorite bed and breakfast. Wake up your loved ones with the familiar smell of maple syrup and spice. Warm their hearts with the memories these unctious dishes made long ago. Fill the air with the aroma of nostalgia and the simple conversation you shared during your first breakfast away from home. Simple and always sweet, nothing says I love you like these morning confections!

> *It is the sweet, simple things of life which are the real ones after all.*
>
> LAURA INGALLS WILDER

Sweetheart Sunrise

MAISON BELIVEAU

Strawberry Cheese Crepe

INGREDIENTS:

For Crepes:

1½ cups flour

1 tbsp sugar

1/2 tsp baking powder

1/2 tsp salt

2 cups milk

2 eggs

1/2 tsp vanilla

2 tbsp melted butter

For Filling:

2 cups ricotta cheese

1/2 cup strawberry jam

For Strawberry Sauce:

1/2 cup strawberry jam

For Lavender Cream:

2 cups heavy whipping cream

1/2 cup confectioner's sugar

1 tsp culinary grade lavender

INSTRUCTIONS:

Measure flour, sugar, baking powder and salt into bowl. Stir in milk, eggs, vanilla, and melted butter.

For each crepe lightly butter 8 inch skillet and heat until bubbly. Pour 1/4 cup batter into skillet rotating to cover pan bottom. Cook until light brown, turn and brown on other side. Crepes may be used immediately or frozen for future use.

For Filling: Mix ricotta cheese with strawberry jam.

For Strawberry Sauce: Melt strawberry jam in microwave until pourable.

For Lavender Cream: Beat heavy whipping cream with confectioner's sugar and lavender, until thick.

Assembly: Fill middle of crepe with 1/3 cup filling. Bring 2 sides up forming log shape. Microwave about 15 seconds. Drizzle heated strawberry sauce over crepe. Place a large dollop of lavender cream on crepe and garnish with fresh strawberries.

NOTES: *Joyce loves lavender and grows this incredible herb at her inn, harvesting the young early culinary grade blossoms and buds.*

YIELD: *6 servings*

Maison Beliveau

5415 Gallion Ridge Rd
Blacksburg, VA
540-961-0505
www.maisonbeliveau.com
Joyce@maisonbeliveau.com

CRYSTAL RIVER INN

Filling for Bananas Foster Crepes

INSTRUCTIONS:
Make a batch 12 large, pretty crepes. This can be done ahead of time. When ready to use, warm them.

Melt butter in a saucepan, then stir in brown sugar. Add enough water to make a thin syrup. Allow to simmer briskly until partly reduced. Add pumpkin pie spice and Grand Marnier or triple sec. Allow to simmer 1–2 minutes, then add bananas and continue to simmer until they wilt, about 5 minutes.

Separately stir together all the ingredients for the topping and set aside.

To assemble, fill each crepe with 4–5 banana slices and wrap it closed, placing seam down on the serving plate. Place a second crepe alongside. Top the twosome with liberal pan syrup, a dollop of crème, toasted almonds, banana slice, and spring of mint. Serve with sausage, Mimosas, and gourmet coffee.

INGREDIENTS:
Filling:

1/4 cup butter, melted

1 cup brown sugar, packed

1 tsp pumpkin pie spice

4 tbsp Grand Marnier or triple sec

3 bananas, sliced

Topping:

1 cup sour cream

2 tbsp whipping cream

1 packet artificial sweetener

Crystal River Inn
326 W Hopkins
San Marcos, TX
512-353-3248
www.crystalriverinn.com
info@crystalriverinn.com

Sweetheart Sunrise

HOLLY HILL HOUSE B&B

Peach and Blueberry Breakfast Pie

INGREDIENTS:

1½ tsp butter

3 large eggs

6 tbsp sugar

1/3 cup cream (half & half or heavy cream)

1 tsp vanilla extract

3 tbsp flour

2 ripe peaches, sliced

3/4 cup fresh or frozen blueberries

powdered sugar

INSTRUCTIONS:

Heat oven to 375 degrees F. Use butter to grease shallow 9 inch pie pan.

Place eggs and sugar in the bowl of an electric mixer and beat until frothy. Add cream, vanilla, and flour and beat until smooth. Pour into buttered pie pan enough batter to coat bottom.

Bake for five minutes. Remove from oven and scatter fruit over batter. Pour remaining batter over it and bake until set 20–25 minutes. Remove from oven—cool 30 minutes—dust with powdered sugar. Cut into wedges and serve. Bon Appétit!

YIELD: *5 servings*

Holly Hill House B&B
611 Polk Street
Port Townsend, WA
360-385-5619
www.hollyhillhouse.com
info@hollyhillhouse.com

No, there's nothing half so sweet in life as love's young dream.

THOMAS MOORE

Inn Love

TAHOMA MEADOWS B&B COTTAGES

Mökki Pannukakku

Tahoma Meadows B&B Cottages
PO Box 234
Tahoma, CA
530-525-1553
www.tahomameadows.com
tahomameadows@sbcglobal.net

NOTE: *The name is Finnish for Cottage Pancake*

INSTRUCTIONS:
Preheat standard oven to 425 degrees F, convection oven to 375 degrees F.

Mix first 6 ingredients in a blender. Don't over mix or your batter will be tough. About 20–30 seconds maximum.

Preparation: Melt butter in 12 inch cast iron skillet. Add optional ingredients and warm them up. You can sauté apples or pears directly in the pan. Pour in batter and sprinkle with brown sugar if desired.

Bake 25–35 minutes until golden brown. Serve with your favorite syrup, jam or powdered sugar and lemon juice.

COOK TIME: *30 min*

INGREDIENTS:

5 eggs

1–2 tbsp sugar, depending on how sweet you want it

2 cups milk

1 cup flour

1 cup cottage cheese

1 tsp baking powder

1/4 cup butter

Options:

1/2 lb cooked breakfast sausage link or loose, drained

Apples or pears, lightly sautéed

Fresh berries or fruit

Cinnamon, nutmeg, cloves, & allspice

Diced ham, lightly sautéed

Sautéed veggies & onions

Toppings: brown sugar, powdered sugar, real maple syrup.

Sweetheart Sunrise

LOVELACE MANOR

Hot Buttered Rum Sauce

INGREDIENTS:

1 stick of butter

1 cup of sugar

2 tbsp of flour

4 tsp of rum

1/2 cup of half & half

Lovelace Manor
2236 Marietta Ave
Lancaster, PA
717-399-3275
www.lovelacemanor.com
hostess@lovelacemanor.com

INSTRUCTIONS:

In a small pot melt 1 stick butter on medium heat, but do not let is start boiling. Mix 1 cup of sugar into the butter, then add 1 tablespoon flour. Stir 1/2 cup half/half into the mixture, keep stirring on medium heat.

The mixture will thicken, as it begins to boil, lower heat to low and let it simmer. Add 4 teaspoons of rum (I like pineapple or coconut rum) and keep the sauce on lowest heat setting just to keep it warm.

Put 1 serving of pancakes on a plate, sprinkle crushed pineapple over the pancakes. Add a section of mandarin orange on top of each pancake. Pour some rum sauce over the pancakes then sprinkle with coconut. Serve with link sausage or bacon.

Inn Love

WARWICK VALLEY BED & BREAKFAST

Baked Whole Wheat Raspberry Pancakes

INGREDIENTS:

2 cups whole wheat flour

1/2 cup natural sugar

1½ tsp baking soda

1 tsp baking powder

2 tbsp canola oil

2 cage free or farm fresh eggs

1 cup raspberries

about 1½ cups fat free milk (antibiotic- and hormone-free)

INSTRUCTIONS:

Mix dry ingredients well add oil, eggs, and milk slowly for consistency a little thicker than to yogurt fold in raspberries.

Use two 9-inch glass Pyrex pie dishes or one large 10×2-inch deep stone pie dish, melt a small amount of butter in each and then divide batter in two. Bake at 350 degrees F on middle shelf for about 30 minutes, rotate after 15 minutes.

Slice like pie and sprinkle a small amount of confectioner's sugar with a drizzle of maple syrup for garnish (a couple raspberries optional).

COOK TIME: *30 min*
YIELD: *6 servings*

Warwick Valley Bed & Breakfast
24 Maple Ave
Warwick, NY
845-987-7255
www.wvbedandbreakfast.com
loretta@warwick.net

Sweetheart Sunrise

WIDOW KIP'S COUNTRY INN

Apple Crisp Pancake

INGREDIENTS:

1 egg beaten

3/4 cup milk

3/4 cup chunky applesauce

1 tsp vanilla

2 cups pancake mix

Topping:

1/2 cup quick oats

1/4 tsp cinnamon

1/4 cup brown sugar

1/2 cup pancake mix

3 tbsp butter

Widow Kip's Country Inn

355 Orchard Dr
Mt. Jackson, VA
540-477-2400
www.widowkips.com
widokips@shentel.net

INSTRUCTIONS:
Spray a jelly roll pan with cooking spray. In a large bowl, combine egg, milk, applesauce, vanilla and pancake mix. Spread the mixture in the prepared pan.

In a medium bowl, combine the oats, brown sugar, pancake mix and butter. Sprinkle the topping over the pancake batter. Bake at 375 degree F oven for 14–16 minutes.

Serve with applesauce and syrup.

COOK TIME: *15 min*

ACADEMY STREET INN
Lemon-Lovers Ricotta Pancakes

INSTRUCTIONS:
Cook on a hot greased griddle like a regular pancake but use a little less batter than you would for a buttermilk pancake.

YIELD: *2 servings*

What is a kiss?

Why this, as some approve:

The sure, sweet cement,

glue, and lime of love.

ROBERT HERRICK

INGREDIENTS:
Whisk:

1 cup part skim ricotta cheese

1 large egg

2 large egg whites

1/2 cup lemon juice

2 tsp grated lemon zest

1 tbsp canola oil

Add to form a thick batter:

1 cup flour

2 tbsp sugar

2 tsp baking powder

1/2 tsp baking soda

1/4 tsp salt

Academy Street Inn
15 Academy St
South Berwick, ME
207-384-5633

CRISANVER HOUSE

Dutch Pancakes

INGREDIENTS:

4 tbsp butter, melted

1 cup all-purpose flour

1 cup milk

4 eggs

4 drops almond extract

INSTRUCTIONS:
Preheat oven to 425 degrees F.

Mix all ingredients well (best with mixer). Heat two 7 inch cast iron skillets while mixing batter. Remove from oven and butter bottom and sides on pan. Pour about 1/4 cup of batter in the preheated pan and bake for 10-12 minutes, until the pancake is brown and very puffy. When you remove from oven it will sink in the center. Cook in 2 batches. You can use any combination of fruit in the center. Sprinkle with powdered sugar and serve with hot maple syrup. You can also fill with scrambled eggs.

COOK TIME: *15 min*
YIELD: *4 servings*

Crisanver House
1434 Crown Point Rd
Shrewsbury, VT
802-492-3589
www.crisanver.com
info@crisanver.com

THE YELLOW HOUSE
Outrageous French Toast

INGREDIENTS:

16 slices inexpensive whole wheat bread, crusts removed

1 cup light brown sugar

1 tbsp light Karo syrup

5 tbsp butter

1 tsp cinnamon

5 eggs

1 ½ cups milk

1 tsp vanilla

sour cream

fresh or frozen strawberries

INSTRUCTIONS:

Over low heat, stir sugar, syrup, cinnamon, and butter until melted and blended. Pour mixture into a 13×9-inch pan, spread evenly on bottom. Place 8 bread slices over mixture, squeezing to fit if necessary. Place remaining 8 slices on top of first 8. Beat eggs with milk and vanilla, pour over bread and refrigerate 8 hours or overnight. Bake in preheated 350 degree F oven for 45 minutes.

To serve, cut into 8 servings, and then flip over onto plate with a spatula, caramelized side up. Put a dollop of sour cream and strawberries on top

COOK TIME: *45 min*
YIELD: *8 servings*

The Yellow House
89 Oakview Dr
Waynesville, NC
828-452-0991
www.theyellowhouse.com
info@theyellowhouse.com

Sweetheart Sunrise

WILLIAMSBURG SAMPLER B&B INN'S
Cheesecake-Stuffed Raspberry French Toast

INGREDIENTS:

1/3 cup of milk

2 tsp vanilla extract

1/3 cup sugar

2 tsp cinnamon

1 egg, beaten

1/3 cup raspberry puree

1½ oz cream cheese, softened

3/8 loaf French bread (cut into 1 inch slices)

butter (to cover large skillet)

confectioner' sugar for dusting

nutmeg (for topping)

Williamsburg Sampler B&B Inn
922 Jamestown Rd
Williamsburg, VA
757-253-0398
www.williamsburgsampler.com
info@williamsburgsampler.com

INSTRUCTIONS:
In a bowl, whisk the milk, vanilla, sugar and cinnamon into the beaten egg until well blended. Set aside. In a separate bowl cream together raspberry puree and cream cheese until smooth. Make sandwich by cutting each slice of bread into half, spreading raspberry-cheese mixture in the center and then topping with the other half.

Melt butter over medium heat in a large skillet (or griddle). Dip bread into egg mixture, coating thoroughly. Cook until well browned on both sides, approximately 5 minutes. Dust with confectioners' sugar and nutmeg (to taste). Serves two. If to your liking adjust recipe to serve additional persons.

YIELD: *2 servings*

CAMEO ROSE VICTORIAN COUNTRY INN

Raspberry Stuffed French Toast

INSTRUCTIONS:

Cut bread into 1½-inch thick slices. Slice a "pocket" in each slice.

Blend Filling: light cream cheese, 2 tablespoon raspberry jam to lightly sweeten, 1/4 cup light ricotta cheese to soften filling.

Beat Batter: 5 fresh extra large eggs, 1 cup heavy whipping cream, 1 teaspoon of pure vanilla extract, 2 tablespoon of sugar, 1 teaspoon cinnamon.

Raspberry Puree Topping: 1 pint fresh raspberries blended and strained into a sauce pan to remove the seeds. Add 1/2 cup water, 1/3 cup sugar, 1 teaspoon of lemon juice. Bring to boil while stirring, and simmer. If necessary, thicken with a small mix of cornstarch & water paste.

To assemble: Spread cream cheese and jam filling in bread pockets. Dip filled bread into the egg batter. Melt some margarine on hot Teflon coated grill heated to 300 degrees F and grill toast about 3 to 3½ minutes per side until golden brown. Cut slices in half. Top with fresh raspberries, a couple tablespoons of sauce, a dollop of whipped cream, and some sliced almonds.

YIELD: *10 large thick slices*
COOK TIME: *20 min*

INGREDIENTS:

almonds, sliced

1 tsp cinnamon

1 package light cream cheese

5 eggs

Italian bread, large loaf

lemon juice

2 pads margarine

1 pint raspberries + extra for garnish

2 tbsp raspberry jam

1/4 cup light ricotta cheese

2 tbsp sugar

1 tsp vanilla extract

water

1 cup heavy whipping cream

Cameo Rose Victorian Country Inn
1090 Severson Rd
Belleville, WI
608-424-6340
www.cameorose.com
innkeeper@cameorose.com

Sweetheart Sunrise

APPLE BLOSSOM INN

Candy Apple French Toast

INGREDIENTS:

1/2 cup (1 stick) butter

1 cup brown sugar

2 tbsp corn syrup

2 tart apples, peeled and sliced

1/4 cup raisins, or try substituting dried cranberries, apricots, cherries, blueberries, etc.

1/4 cup chopped walnuts, or try substituting pecans, almonds, Macadamias, etc.

1 loaf sweet French bread, cut into 1-inch slices

5 eggs

1¼ cups milk

1 tsp vanilla extract

Sugar-Cinnamon topping:

3 tbsp sugar

1½ tsp ground cinnamon

Seasonal fruits

Apple Blossom Inn
44606 Silver Spur Trl
Ahwahnee, CA
559-642-2001
www.appleblossombb.com
appleblossominn@sti.net

INSTRUCTIONS:

Cook butter, sugar and corn syrup in saucepan over medium heat until it thickens to a syrup consistency. Pour into 9×13-inch baking dish that has been prepared with cooking spray. Spread apple slices, dried fruit and nuts over syrup. Place bread on top. Whisk together eggs, milk and vanilla. Pour over bread. Cover and refrigerate overnight. Before baking, preheat oven to 350 degrees F. Sprinkle top with mixture of sugar and cinnamon. Bake, uncovered, for 40–45 minutes.

Remove from oven and allow to cool for 5 minutes. Invert onto a platter (be very careful as it is extremely HOT).

Arrange a variety of colorful seasonal fruits (such as strawberries, melons, raspberries, blueberries, kiwis, etc.) around the French toast and enjoy!

Inn Love

BOTTGER MANSION OF OLD TOWN

Berry Good French Toast

INSTRUCTIONS:

Grease a 9×13-inch baking dish. Place milk, sugar, vanilla, salt, cinnamon, nutmeg, and eggs in a large bowl and beat with a hand-mixer until smooth. Add bread cubes and stir with a spoon until coated.

Pour bread mixture into pan. Top evenly with cream cheese, blueberries and pecans. Cover and refrigerate up to 24 hours.

Heat oven to 400 degrees F. Bake uncovered 20–25 minutes or until golden brown. Cut into servings. Dust with powdered sugar and serve with maple syrup.

COOK TIME: *30 min*

INGREDIENTS:

14 oz milk

1/4 cup sugar

1 tsp vanilla

1/4 tsp salt

2 tsp cinnamon

1 tsp nutmeg

7 large eggs

16 oz loaf French bread, cut into 1" cubes

3 oz cream cheese, cut into 1/2" cubes

1 cup fresh or frozen blueberries

1/2 cup chopped pecans

Bottger Mansion of Old Town
110 San Felipe NW
Albuquerque, NM
505-243-3639
www.bottger.com
info@bottger.com

Sweetheart Sunrise

TIDEWATER INN

Cranberry-Almond French Toast Souffle

FILLING:

1 (8-oz) pkg cream cheese, at room temperature

8 large eggs

1/2 tsp vanilla extract

1½ cup 2% milk

2/3 cup half & half

1/2 cup maple syrup (grade B)

1 loaf Challah bread (22 oz)

1/2 cup craisins (dried cranberries)

2 tbsp sliced almonds

Powdered Sugar, for garnish

Maple Syrup, warmed, to serve with

Tidewater Inn
949 Boston Post Rd
Madison, CT
203-245-8457
www.TheTidewater.com
escape@thetidewater.com

INSTRUCTIONS:
Preheat oven to 375 degrees F.

In a very large bowl, beat cream cheese until smooth. Add eggs, 1 at a time, mixing well after each addition. Add vanilla extract, milk, half & half and maple syrup and mix until smooth. Cut bread into 3/4" cubes and add to batter. Add craisins. Mix well with a large mixing spoon until all the liquid is absorbed by the bread.

Spray a 9×13-inch glass baking dish with cooking spray. Spoon French toast soufflé mixture into the dish and distribute evenly. Sprinkle sliced almonds over all. Bake for 45 to 60 minutes, until center is set and all is golden brown. Sprinkle with powdered sugar to serve, and enjoy with warmed maple syrup.

COOK TIME: *50 min*
YIELD: *10 servings*

Inn Love

OLD MONTEREY INN

Orange Blossom French Toast

INSTRUCTIONS:

Mix the first six ingredients together in a blender. This mixture may be made the evening before use; blend before using. Preheat oven to 350 degrees F.

Use pre-cut loaves of sweet French bread (Texas toast) or any thick sliced bread of your liking. Remove crusts and slice each on a diagonal (1½ full slices per person is what we serve, you might like to use two full slices per person).

Dip in batter, let excess drip off. Roll in corn flake crumbs, sprinkle with dried orange peel and place on greased baking sheet.

Bake at 350 degrees F for 25 minutes. Bake 5 minutes, brush with melted butter if you wish. This will make the toast a little more crisp.

Serve with slices of oranges and maple or marmalade syrup.

COOK TIME: *25 min*
YIELD: *2 servings*

INGREDIENTS:

2 eggs

1/4 cup milk

1/4 cup orange juice

1/8 tsp salt

1 dash cinnamon

1/2 tbsp orange extract

3 or 4 slices of bread

1+ cups of corflake crumbs

Old Monterey Inn
500 Martin St
Monterey, CA
831-375-8284
www.oldmontereyinn.com
omi@oldmontereyinn.com

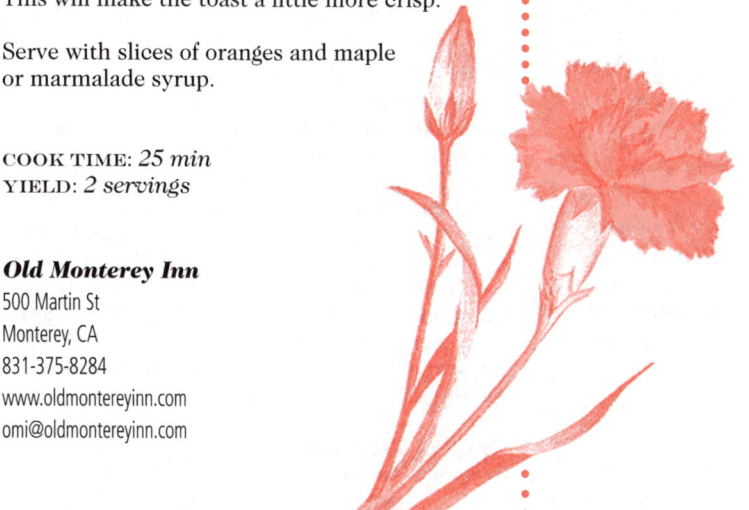

Sweetheart Sunrise

PELICAN COVE INN

Carmel Apple French Toast

INGREDIENTS:

1/2 cup butter

1 cup brown sugar

2 tbsp light corn syrup

1 cup chopped pecans

12 slices sweet French bread (not sourdough)

6 to 8 green apples, peeled and thinly sliced

6 eggs

1½ cups milk

1 tsp vanilla extract

1/2 tsp ground cinnamon

1/8 tsp ground nutmeg

Pelican Cove Inn
320 Walnut Ave
Carlsbad, CA
760-434-5995
www.pelican-cove.com
PelicanCoveInn@pelican-cove.com

Love planted a rose, and the world turned sweet.

KATHARINE LEE BATES

INSTRUCTIONS:
In a small saucepan mix butter, brown sugar and corn syrup over medium heat; stirring constantly until thickened. Grease 13×9-inch pan and pour mixture into the bottom of the pan. Arrange bread slices over the caramel mixture; top with apple slices. Mix eggs, milk and vanilla together and pour over apples. Sprinkle with cinnamon and nutmeg. Cover and put in refrigerator overnight. In the morning, preheat oven to 350 and bake for 50 to 60 minutes. Sprinkle with nuts and serve with whipped cream.

YIELD: *8 servings*
COOK TIME: *50 min*

GOODBREAD HOUSE

"Temptation" Apple Baked French Toast

INSTRUCTIONS:

The night before serving, fill the bottom of two 9×9-inch pans with half the bread cubes. Layer the cream cheese first, then the apple pie filling. Top with sliced real apples followed by raisins. Add remaining bread cubes on top.

Beat egg, maple syrup, and milk together. Pour mixture evenly over both pans of bread. Cover and refrigerate overnight. Bake uncovered at 350 degrees F for 45 minutes or until lightly browned. After 20 minutes, garnish with pecan pieces. Allow to cool. Top with caramel flavored whipped cream (optional).

YIELD: *12 servings*
COOK TIME: *45 min*

Sweet things happen. They still do.

DIANNE WIEST

INGREDIENTS:

1½ loaves French bread, cubed

2 (8 oz) packages of cream cheese, softened

1 dozen large eggs

3/4 cups maple syrup

1 cup milk

2 (21-oz) cans apple pie filling

1 cup raisins

pecan pieces, for garnish

Goodbread House
209 Osborne St
St. Marys, GA
912-882-7490
www.goodbreadhouse.com
info@goodbreadhouse.com

Sweetheart Sunrise

LOGANBERRY INN

Crème Brulee French Toast

INGREDIENTS:

2 tbsp corn syrup (light or dark)

1/2 cup butter (1 stick)

1 cup brown sugar, packed

1 loaf French or white bread, thickly sliced, with the crust removed

5 eggs

1½ cups half & half, or half milk & half cream

1 tsp vanilla

1 tsp Grand Marnier or orange baking liqueur, 70% alcohol (optional)

1/4 tsp salt

Loganberry Inn
310 W 7th St
Fulton, MO
573-642-9229
www.loganberryinn.com
info@loganberryinn.com

INSTRUCTIONS:

In a small saucepan combine the syrup, butter and brown sugar; simmer until syrupy. Pour this mixture into a 9×13-inch baking pan that has been sprayed with Pam non-stick spray. Set aside.

Slice the loaf into thick slices, and place the syrup in the baking pan. Place the bread on top of the syrup.

In a large bowl, whisk together the eggs, cream, vanilla, Grand Marnier and salt. Pour evenly over the bread. Cover and refrigerate overnight.

In the morning, leave the casserole at room temperature while the oven preheats. Bake at 350 degrees F uncovered, for 45 minutes. Cut into squares and serve immediately. Serve with maple syrup and butter. Can be reheated.

NOTE: *Cathy is a Celebrity Chef at Dierbergs Cooking Schools in St. Louis.*

J. PAULES' FENN INN
Stuffed French Toast

INSTRUCTIONS:

The French toast must be prepared the night before, then bake just before serving.

Grease a 13×9×2-inch glass baking dish. Spread the cream cheese over half of the bread slices. Cover with the remaining slices to make sandwiches. Remove the crusts and cut into 1 inch cubes. Place in the prepared baking dish.

Mix the eggs, cream, maple syrup, pancake mix and butter until well blended. Pour evenly over the bread, press the bread down until it soaks up the egg mixture. Cover and refrigerate for a least 8 hours, or overnight.

Preheat the oven to 350 degrees F. Bake uncovered for 40 to 60 minutes (60 minutes for a double batch)or until lightly browned.

Meanwhile, make the sauce: Heat the strawberries and strawberry preserves in a saucepan, stirring gently, until the preserves have melted. Cut the French toast into squares and serve warm, with the strawberry sauce. Makes about 3 ½ cups of strawberry sauce.

You should be able to insert a knife in the center and it should come out clean if done.

NOTE: *If you double the recipe, do not double the butter, still use 1/2 cup)*

COOK TIME: *50 min*
YIELD: *10 servings*

INGREDIENTS:

8 oz cream cheese

1½ pound loaf firm white bread (about 16 slices)

12 eggs

1½ cups half & half

1/4 cup maple syrup

1/2 cup butter, melted

1/4 cup pancake mix

Strawberry Sauce:

2 cups sliced fresh strawberries (1 pint)

2 cups strawberry preserves

J. Paules' Fenn Inn
2254 S 58th St
Fennville, MI
269-561-2836
www.jpaulesfenninn.com
jpaules@accn.org

Sweetheart Sunrise

BARCLAY COTTAGE BED AND BREAKFAST'S

Baked French Toast

INGREDIENTS:

12 large eggs

1½ cups milk

1½ tsp vanilla

1 heaping tsp butterscotch pudding mix

1 loaf Italian, French, Portuguese or similar bread

1 cup light brown sugar

1/4 lb butter (1 stick)

2 tbsp maple syrup

1/2 tsp cinnamon

1 dash nutmeg

Barclay Cottage Bed and Breakfast
400 16th St
Virginia Beach, VA
757-422-1956
www.barclaycottage.com
innkeepers@barclaycottage.com

INSTRUCTIONS:
Slice bread diagonally into 3/4- to 1-inch slices (16 for 8 people).

Blend: eggs, milk, vanilla, and pudding mix and soak bread in mixture until absorbed. Arrange wet bread slices in 9×13-inch greased pan so they overlap each other slightly.

Melt together: brown sugar, butter, maple syrup, cinnamon and nutmeg and pour over bread so that it is evenly distributed between the slices. Cover and refrigerate overnight. Bake uncovered at 375 degrees F for 50 minutes. Sprinkle with pecans and sliced bananas. Serve with warm maple syrup and bacon or sausage.

NOTE: *Optional: Arrange thinly sliced apple slices between each slice of bread before covering with melted butter/brown sugar mix*

COOK TIME: *50 min*
YIELD: *6 servings*

Inn Love

PLEASANT LAKE B&B

Honey Baked French Toast

INSTRUCTIONS:

Slice bread diagonally into 12 slices. Grease 9×13-inch pan. In a small bowl, beat eggs, milk, cinnamon and 2 tablespoons honey, till smooth. Dip bread slices in egg mixture & place in pan forming 3 rows overlapping slightly. Pour any remaining egg mixture over the top. Cover & refrigerate overnight.

In the morning, sprinkle with brown sugar, drizzle with 2 tablespoons honey & melted butter. Bake at 350 degrees F for 30 minutes. Serve with warm maple syrup.

YIELD: *6 servings*

Life is one grand, sweet song, so start the music.

RONALD REAGAN

INGREDIENTS:

1 loaf French bread

4 eggs

1¼ cups milk

1 tsp cinnamon

4 tbsp honey, divided

3 tbsp brown sugar

2 tbsp butter, melted

Pleasant Lake B&B

2238 60th Ave

Osceola, WI

715-294-2545

www.pleasantlake.com

plakebb@centurytel.net

Sweetheart Sunrise

THE COLONEL TAYLOR INN BED & BREAKFAST

Holiday Morning French Toast

INGREDIENTS:

1 cup brown sugar

1/2 cup butter, melted

3 tsp cinnamon

3 Granny Smith apples, peeled, cored & thinly sliced

1/2 cup dried cranberries

1 loaf Italian bread cut into 1" slices

6 large eggs

1½ cup milk

1 tbsp vanilla

INSTRUCTIONS:

Combine brown sugar, butter & 1 tsp cinnamon in a 13×9-inch baking dish. Add apples & cranberries: toss to coat well. Spread mixture evenly over bottom of baking dish. Arrange slices of bread on top.

Mix eggs, milk, vanilla & remaining 2 tsp of cinnamon until well blended. Pour mixture over bread, soaking bread completely. Cover & refrigerate 4 to 24 hours.

Bake, covered with aluminum foil, in a preheated 375 degrees F oven for 40 minutes. Uncover & bake 5 minutes. Remove from oven; let stand for 5 minutes. Serve warm with maple syrup.

COOK TIME: *45 min*

The Colonel Taylor Inn Bed & Breakfast
633 Upland Rd
Cambridge, OH
740-432-7802
www.coltaylorinnbb.com
coltaylor@coltaylorinnbb.com

RED BLUFF COTTAGE
Wild Rice Waffles

INSTRUCTIONS:

In a large bowl, toss wild rice and cherries. Add dry ingredients and continue to toss making sure rice and cherries are well coated.

Separate eggs. Combine egg yolks and buttermilk. Add to wild rice mixture. Add melted butter. Beat egg whites and fold into batter.

Ladle waffles onto preheated waffle iron and cook until golden brown and slightly crisp. Finished waffles may be kept warm in 200 degree F oven or in a warming tray while the remaining batter is prepared.

Serve hot with whipping cream, fresh Alabama peaches (and/or other seasonal fresh fruits, such as, strawberries, raspberries, blueberries, pineapple, blackberries and bananas) and warm maple syrup. Makes 8 waffles.

NOTE: *We prepare the rice ahead of time as directed on the package and freeze the portion size needed for each recipe. Batter can be made several hours ahead and refrigerated. It also freezes well. Frozen batter may be thawed in the refrigerator one day.*

YIELD: *8 servings*

INGREDIENTS:

1 cup all-purpose flour

1 cup whole wheat flour

3½ cup cooked wild rice, well drained

2/3 cup dried cherries (or dried cranberries)

4 tbsp sugar

4 tsp baking powder

1 tsp baking soda

1/2 tsp salt

2½ cup buttermilk

4 large eggs

1/2 cup (1 stick) unsalted butter, melted

Red Bluff Cottage
551 Clay St
Montgomery, AL
334-264-0056
www.redbluffcottage.com
info@redbluffcottage.com

Enticing Side Dishes

LIKE YOU AND YOUR SWEETHEART, some dishes complement one another spectacularly, and add that extra pizazz to any meal. These appetizing accompaniments perfect any meal, completing any course with the elegance of your favorite bed and breakfast menu. But these recipes aren't just a garnish – they can be a tasty meal (or snack!) by themselves. Aside from being sides, they're great on their own, and can be savored from dusk till dawn. Whether you choose to make a warm bowl of soup for a cool night or a crisp fruit salad for a summer picnic, these recipes are sure to please your's and your partners' palate.

Let us celebrate the occasion with wine and sweet words.

PLAUTUS

Enticing Side Dishes

EDELWEISS MANOR
Berry Cooler

INGREDIENTS:

2 quarts of berry juice (mixed or single berry)

1 large can frozen white grape juice

1 liter club soda

INGREDIENTS:

Mix together, sweeten to taste, chill and serve.

Rim Decor: Mix 2 Tbsp of berry juice and 1/4 cup of granulated sugar. Mix, dip goblet in water to moisten, and then dip rims in sugar.

NOTE: *When we serve this at Edelweiss Manor, we prefer to use our own fresh pressed Nectar-berry Juice. The result is a beautifully colored, rich beverage.*

Edelweiss Manor
1708 NW Springhill Dr.
Albany, OR
541-928-0747
www.edelweissmanor.com
info@edelweissmanor.com

Love is

the flower

you've got to

let grow.

JOHN LENNON

Inn Love

CREEKSIDE B&B

Carmelized Bacon

INGREDIENTS:

1 lb thick sliced bacon

1/2 cup brown sugar

1/2 tsp cayenne pepper

2 tbsp water

Creekside B&B
5325 Vineyard Dr
Paso Robles, CA
805-227-6585
www.thecreeksidebb.com
LTeckman@percazocellars.com

INSTRUCTIONS:
Stir flour, sugar and salt in large bowl.

Preheat oven to 375 degrees F.

Combine sugar, pepper and water. Line a large baking sheet with foil. Top with a rack and spray with PAM. Place sliced bacon on rack and baste the mixture on each slice of bacon. Bake for 25–30 minutes to your crispness preference.

COOK TIME: *25 min*

Enticing Side Dishes

INN AT VALLEY FARMS B&B & COTTAGES
Strawberry Rhubarb Compote

INGREDIENTS:

1 cup sugar

2" piece of ginger, peeled and quartered

1 lb fresh local rhubarb, cut into 1½" pieces

1 tbsp orange zest

1 pint fresh local strawberries, hulled and halved

fresh local cream

fresh sprigs of chocolate mint or peppermint

Inn at Valley Farms B&B & Cottages
633 Wentworth Rd
Walpole, NH
603-756-2855
www.innatvalleyfarms.com
info@innatvalleyfarms.com

INSTRUCTIONS:
Bring the water, sugar and ginger to a boil in a heavy saucepan over medium heat. Add the rhubarb, bring back to a boil, then lower the heat. Partially cover and simmer for several minutes or until rhubarb is soft but retains its shape. Remove from heat. Let cool for a couple of minutes then stir in orange zest and strawberries. Chill. Remove ginger before serving.

Serve in stemmed glasses with a splash of fresh local cream and topped with a sprig of fresh mint.

NOTE: *I serve it as a first course for breakfast to our inn guests in a stemmed crystal glass, but it's equally as good for dessert served over locally made Walpole Creamery vanilla ice cream or as a topping for homemade cheesecake. Very simple and delicious.*

HAYDON STREET INN

Candied Walnuts

INSTRUCTIONS:
Mix cinnamon, cayenne, salt, simple syrup and walnuts in a large sauce pan. Bring to a boil then simmer for 15 minutes, stirring occasionally. Drain well and spread on oiled baking sheet. Generously sprinkle with turbinado sugar. Bake at 225 degrees F for 2½ hours. Stir after 1 hour continue baking for 1½ hours, turn off oven and let cool in oven over night if possible. These will keep well in zipper plastic bags.

COOK TIME: *4 hrs*
YIELD: *4 cups*

INGREDIENTS:

- 1 lb walnuts (can substitute any nut)
- 1 tbsp ground cinnamon
- 2 quarts simple syrup (equal parts of sugar and water)
- 1 cup turbinado or coarse grind sugar
- 1 tsp ground cayenne pepper (optional)

Haydon Street Inn
321 Haydon St
Healdsburg, CA
707-433-5228
www.haydon.com
innkeeper@haydon.com

Enticing Side Dishes

ADAMS BASIN INN

Chilled Creamy Peach Soup

INGREDIENTS:

4–5 fresh ripe peaches (1 extra for garnish)

1/2 cup orange juice

3 tbsp sugar

dash of cinnamon

1/4 cup sour cream

2 tbsp triple-sec (optional)

INSTRUCTIONS:

Peel peaches, place in blender with orange juice. Pulse until pureed. Add sugar and cinnamon, pulse until well blended. Add sour cream and pulse again. Add triple-sec pulse again. Refrigerate until ready to serve, no more than 30 minutes to an hour.

NOTE: *Serve in large martini glasses with slices of fresh peaches, mint leaf and a dollop of whipping cream or crème fraiche. Great!!!*

YIELD: *4 servings*

Adams Basin Inn
PO Box 830
Adams Basin, NY
585-352-3999
www.adamsbasininn.com
hainespat@gmail.com

IVY CREEK FARM

Strawberry Balsamic Soup

INSTRUCTIONS:

For the soup: In a large bowl, mix the strawberries, sugar, vinegar, orange and lemon zests and Grand Marnier. Set aside until the sugar has dissolved, about 5 minutes. In a food processor or blender, process ingredients until smooth (may have to work in batches).

In a large bowl using a spatula or wooden spoon, stir the yogurt until it reaches an even consistency. Add the strawberry puree and stir until completely combined and no streaks remain. Cover and refrigerate until chilled through, at least 2 hours. Will keep longer.

For the garnish: In a bowl, toss the strawberries with the sugar and vinegar. Macerate by refrigerating or setting aside at room temperature for at least 2 hours.

Just prior to serving, ladle the soup into individual bowls. Top each bowl with several of the macerated strawberries and drizzle with the syrup that remains in the bottom of the bowl from the macerated strawberries. Serve immediately after garnishing.

YIELD: *12 cups*

Ivy Creek Farm
2812 Link Rd
Lynchburg, VA
434-384-3802
www.ivycreekfarm.com
info@ivycreekfarm.com

INGREDIENTS:

For the soup:

1 quart strawberries, hulled

1 cup granulated sugar

6 tbsp balsamic vinegar

1/2 tsp grated orange zest

1/2 tsp grated lemon zest

1 tbsp Grand Marnier or other orange-flavored liqueur

6 cups plain yogurt (may use low-fat or nonfat)

For the garnish:

20 strawberries, hulled and halved

1/2 cup granulated sugar

2 tbsp balsamic vinegar

Enticing Side Dishes

CARRIAGE HOUSE B&B'S
Broccoli Potato Soup

INGREDIENTS:

16 oz bag of chopped broccoli

2 cups chicken broth

2 cans cream of potato soup

2 cups milk

1 cup grated Velveeta cheese (or more, to taste)

INSTRUCTIONS:
Boil broccoli and broth for 8 minutes, then reduce heat. Add cream of potato soup and milk. Warm gently until soup is hot, but not boiling. Add Velveeta cheese, stir to melt cheese. Ready to serve!

COOK TIME: *20 min*
YIELD: *4 servings*

Carriage House B&B
1133 Broad St
Grinnell, IA
641-236-7520
www.ia-bednbreakfast-inns.com/carriagehousegrinnell.htm
irishbnb@iowatelecom.net

Love is life.

And if you

miss love, you

miss life.

LEO BUSCAGLIA

LA MAISON DE LUCY

Lucy's French Onion Soup

INSTRUCTIONS:
Slice French baguette into thin slices and put under 375 degree F oven. Watch carefully until French baguette is nice and toasted. Set aside.

Melt butter in the bottom of an oven-safe large pot or Dutch oven. Add onions and sprinkle with sugar. Sauté in bottom of pan until nice and soft and caramelized/golden in color. After onions are golden in color, add hot water to cover the onions. Add the flour mixture* into the soup to thicken it, whisking to make sure there are no clumps. Add salt and pepper, then turn down burner to a low heat and let cook for a at least 20 more minutes (soup can cook on low heat as long as you like).

For the flour mixture, it is important to get a separate bowl, add some soup from the batch, and slowly whisk the flour into that smaller amount of soup. After flour is all mixed in and there are no flour clumps, add that back into the large pot of soup and mix in.

In a separate bowl, mix together the egg yolk and Porto. When the soup is ready, mix the egg and Porto mixture into the pot of soup. Take the baguette pieces and put on the top of the soup. Spread cheese liberally over the baguette. Put entire dish into the oven at about 400 degrees under the broiler. Watch carefully, and take out when cheese in nice and melted, and browning on the top (about 5–7 minutes).

VARIATION: *You can also serve the soup in individual ramekins. Make the soup as listed above, but put the soup into individual oven-safe ramekins before putting under the broiler. Add the baguette and cheese and put into the oven under broiler as directed above.*

INGREDIENTS:

1 French baguette

butter
(about 1–2 tbsp)

6 onions, sliced very thinly

1 liberal tsp sugar

salt and pepper, to taste

1 tbsp flour

hot water

1 egg yolk

2 tbsp Porto

cheese (Gruyere is preferred but you can use any cheese)

COOK TIME:
30 min
YIELD:
6 servings

La Maison de Lucy
2388 Park Avenue
Alford, FL
850-579-0138
www.lamaisondelucy.com
lamaisondelucy@yahoo.com

Enticing Side Dishes

CANYON FERRY MANSION

Three Cheese Creamy Champagne

INGREDIENTS:

1 can Carnation milk unsweetened

1/2 cup Kraft Parmesan cheese

1/4 lb Kraft Velveeta cheese

1/2 cup grated cheddar cheese any style *(medium is our favorite)*

INSTRUCTIONS:
Mix, melt and stir with wire whip all together first group of ingredients until creamy in microwave about 3 minutes, then again till blended.

Blend the second group of ingredients in food processor with blunt short blade until just blended with on/off strokes.

NOTE: Broccoli should be not more than 1/4-inch pieces. This is the secret to taking out that strong frozen broccoli taste and bringing back the sweetness of fresh picked.

Add broccoli mixture to milk & cheese mixture along with Champagne. Stir with wire whip and heat about 3 more minutes. Whip again until cheese & Champagne base is smooth.

Bid me to love, and I will give a loving heart to thee.

ROBERT HERRICK

104 *Inn Love*

Broccoli Soup

1 lb or 1 package frozen chopped or blanched frozen broccoli chopped from garden (use only tender heads not lower stalks

1 tbsp chopped garlic - jar type

2 tbsp butter

4 dashes of sea salt

1 scant dash white pepper

2 dashes black pepper

1/2 tsp chicken bouillon or 1 cube

1½ cups of left over flat Champagne

NOTE: Taste and adjust salt & pepper if needed. Spoon into cups. Reheat gently if needed when guests come in.

Canyon Ferry Mansion
7408 Hwy 287 N
Townsend, MT
www.canyonferrymansion.com
Sandy@canyonferrymansion.com

Enticing Side Dishes

THE MAINE STAY INN

Gingered Fruit Salad

INGREDIENTS:

1/3 cup lime juice

1/3 cup water

1/3 cup sugar

whole pineapple, cut into cubes

blueberries

1/4 cup crystallized ginger, finely chopped

Granny Smith apples

The Maine Stay Inn
PO Box 500A
Kennebunkport, ME
207-967-2117
www.mainestayinn.com
innkeeper@mainestayinn.com

INSTRUCTIONS:
Preheat oven to 350F.

Bring sugar, water, and lime juice to a boil in a small saucepan. Stir until sugar is dissolved. Remove from heat and cool to room temperature. Toss fruit in lime sauce and sprinkle with chopped ginger.

NOTE: *The yield for this recipe depends on you. The chef can be creative and add mangoes instead of apples, if they are available and desirable. I generally use about 3 cups of blueberries, and add other fruits to make the mixture seem balanced.*

COOK TIME: *30 min*

MAISON LAVIGNE

Fruit Salade Vinaigrette

INSTRUCTIONS:

Make the vinaigrette by smashing the garlic and the basil leaves together with the mustard, salt, pepper and sugar as if making a pesto. When very well mashed, add the vinegar and blend well. Drizzle in the olive oil, blending to make a vinaigrette.

Slice strawberries and mix together with washed and dried grapes, and orange segments. Add 1/2 of the vinaigrette. Delicately stir the vinaigrette throughout the fruits. In a separate bowl, place 1/4 of the vinaigrette with the arugula and toss gently to coat the lettuces. Place altogether on a platter with the fruits and serve with quiche. Also great in little fruit cups making it easy to get to the grapes.

COOK TIME: *20 min*
YIELD: *8 servings*

Maison LaVigne
3532 South Fulton Avenue
Hapeville, GA
404-766-5561
www.maisonlavigne.com
atableoffriends@aol.com

INGREDIENTS:

1 lb Driscoll strawberries

1/2 lb green grapes

1/2 lb red grapes

1 lb arugula

2 cups fresh orange segments or drained canned Mandarins

5 fresh basil leaves

1/2 tsp Dijon mustard

1/2 tsp Mediterranean sea salt

1/2 tsp peppercorn medley, ground

1/8 tsp Sugar in the Raw

1 fresh garlic clove

1/4 cup Alessi Raspberry Blush White Balsamic Vinegar

3/4 cup Spanish extra virgin olive oil

Enticing Side Dishes

TALKEETNA ROADHOUSE

Garlic Herb Vinaigrette

INGREDIENTS:

22 scallions

11 cloves garlic

1 tsp black pepper

1 tbsp basil

1 tbsp dry mustard

1 tbsp oregano

1 tbsp dry dill weed

1/2 tsp celery seed

3½ cups olive oil

3½ cups rice wine vinegar

3/4 cups orange juice

INSTRUCTIONS:

Wash then rough chop scallions. Chop garlic and place both scallions and garlic in food processor. Add all dry spices. Measure the liquids into one container; pour slowly into food processor while processing. Process in batches so as not to overflow food processor.

NOTE: *This is outstanding on salads and works very nicely as a marinade for chicken or for salmon. We also coat our croutons and bagel chips with this dressing for great flavor.*

YIELD: *8 cups*

Talkeetna Roadhouse
PO Box 604
Talkeetna, AK
907-733-1351
www.talkeetnaroadhouse.com
reservations@talkeetnaroadhouse.com

Idleness, like kisses, to be sweet must be stolen.

JEROME K. JEROME

THE IRISH INN

Romaine Orange Salad

INGREDIENTS:

1/4 cup extra virgin oil

1 large onion, peeled and diced

2 tbsp sugar

3 tbsp white vinegar

1 tsp chopped fresh basil

1 tbsp low sodium soy sauce

1/2 cup raw cashews

1 can drained Mandarin orange sections

1 head very fresh romaine lettuce

1/2 small ball fresh mozzarella cheese, cubed

1 large tomato, diced

INSTRUCTIONS:
Heat olive oil until hot, but not smoking. Add onions, and cook until translucent and aromatic. Add raw cashews and soy sauce, and cook until they turn light brown. Sprinkle sugar, basil, and vinegar over mixture in pan, turning quickly.

Remove from heat, and chill for one hour. Mix with romaine, tomato, and Mozzarella thoroughly. Add Mandarin oranges, and toss once more lightly before serving.

YIELD: *4 serving*

The Irish Inn
PO Box 97
Ozark, IL
618-695-3355
irishinn.tripod.com
dalianmoore@yahoo.com

Enticing Side Dishes

GRAND LIVING B&B

Fresh Pineapple Ambrosia

INGREDIENTS:

2 cups fresh pineapple chunks

1 can (11-oz) Mandarin orange segments, drained

1 cup Jet-Puffed Miniature Marshmallows

1 banana, sliced

1/2 cup flake coconut, toasted

INSTRUCTIONS:

Mix all ingredients in a large bowl. Serve immediately.

COOK TIME: *10 min*
YIELD: *8 servings*

Grand Living B&B
701 Quarterhorse Rd
Williams, AZ
928-635-4171
www.grandlivingbnb.com
job@grandlivingbnb.com

OAK COVE
Spinach Parmesan

INGREDIENTS:

1 (10-oz) package chopped spinach

2 eggs

1/2 cup Parmesan cheese

1 cup cottage cheese

1/2 tsp salt

Oak Cove
58881 46th St
Lawrence, MI
269-674-8228
www.oakcove.com
oakcove@hughes.net

INSTRUCTIONS:
Preheat oven to 350 degrees F.

Cook the spinach and drain well. Add the eggs, Parmesan, cottage cheese, and salt; mix and bake in a small pan (8×8-inch) for 1 hour.

NOTE: *This is lovely for Fish Florentine. Roll fish around a hand full of spinach Parmesan and cook until done. Sprinkle with paprika.*

COOK TIME: *1 hr*
YIELD: *4 servings*

Enticing Side Dishes

HICKORY BRIDGE FARM
Summer Squash

INGREDIENTS:

2 medium-size yellow squash

1 tbsp sliced onion

1 tsp salt

1 tsp pepper

2 tbsp butter or margarine

2 tbsp light brown sugar

Hickory Bridge Farm
96 Hickory Bridge Rd
Orrtanna, PA
717-642-5261
www.hickorybridgefarm.com
info@hickorybridgefarm.com

INSTRUCTIONS:
Slice squash into large saucepan, remove large seeds. Chop onion on top; add 1/2 cup water, salt, and pepper. Cook over medium heat with lid on pan. Stir a few times to prevent sticking. When squash is "fork tender", add butter and brown sugar. Do not overcook.

A simple enough pleasure, surely, to have breakfast alone with one's husband, but how seldom married people in the midst of life achieve it.

ANNE SPENCER

Enticing Side Dishes 113

Alluring Appetizers

INTRIGUE YOUR TASTE BUDS with these tempting tidbits. Recall the unique spread of treats offered by that fantastic inn of your dreams. Taste once again that delicate appetizer, that elegant morsel that warmed your palate and prompted conversation. Share that memory through a simple dinner for two, or indulge in variety and host a tapas party complete with your favorite wine. Give your friends and loved ones something they will chatter about for days through these succulent starts.

I can resist everything except temptation.

OSCAR WILDE

STONEHURST PLACE'S
Cheese Straws

INGREDIENTS

1/2 lb (2 sticks) organic unsalted butter, softened

1 lb extra-sharp cheddar cheese, finely shredded

2 cups organic all-purpose flour

1 tsp fine sea salt

1/4 tsp red cayenne pepper

Stonehurst Place
923 Piedmont Ave NE
Atlanta, GA
404-881-0722
www.StonehurstPlace.com
info@StonehurstPlace.com

INSTRUCTIONS:
Preheat oven to 350 degrees.

Cream the butter and cheese in food processor until smooth. By hand, work in flour, salt and pepper. Roll into a 12-inch log; wrap in plastic wrap and chill overnight.

Remove dough log from refrigerator and let soften until it can be placed into the tube of a cookie press. Fit the cookie press with a star or straw tip. Press long strips of the mixture onto an ungreased cookie sheet.

Bake straws at 350 degrees F for 8–12 minutes, until crisp and very lightly browned. Remove from oven and score long strips into individual straws approximately 3 inch long. Let straws sit for 1–2 minutes until firm enough to transfer to wire racks for cooling; separate into individual 3 inch straws at transfer. Serve at room temperature.

Store baked cheese straws in an airtight container for up to one week. The dough may be frozen in small batches, thawed and baked for fresh straws. Very rich, but sure of success!

VARIATION: Use 1 pound hot pepper cheese mixed with 1 pound sharp cheddar for a spicier cheese straw.

COOK TIME: *15 min*
YIELD: *5 dozen*

LODGE AT SEDONA
Pear, Walnut and Blue Cheese Flat Bread

INSTRUCTIONS:
Preheat oven to 450°F.

Dough: Mix yeast, 1 teaspoon sugar and water together and set aside. Put flour, 1/2 tablespoon salt, 2 teaspoons sugar, walnuts and olive oil in food processor and mix. When yeast has foam on top, add to food processor and process until it comes together. This is enough kneading. Put dough in a well-oiled bowl and cover with plastic wrap. Allow to rise for 1 hour. Prepare a full sheet pan with Pam, oil spray, and sprinkle with corn meal. Press dough on pan.

Toppings: Spread pear puree on dough. Top with cheeses, walnuts and rosemary. Bake for 15 minutes or until the cheeses have melted and browned slightly.

Garnish & Presentation: Cut flat bread in 1" × 1" squares and serve on a platter. Can be served with herbed olive oil or a stilton and garlic spread.

COOK TIME: *15 min*
YIELD: *1/2 sheet pan*

Lodge at Sedona
125 Kallof Place
Sedoona, AZ
928-204-1942
ww.LODGEatSEDONA.com
info@lodgeatsedona.com

INGREDIENTS:
Dough:

1 tbsp dry active yeast

1½ cup warm water

3 cup all-purpose flour

2 tsp sugar

1/2 tbsp salt

1/2 cup chopped walnuts

2 tbsp olive oil

1 large egg

Topping:

2 cups pears, pureed

3 oz blue cheese crumbles

1/2 cup walnuts

1 cup jack cheese

1 tbsp chopped rosemary

Alluring Appetizers

ELLIOTT HOUSE

Baked Wonton Cups

INGREDIENTS:

Filling:

2 green onions

3 oz cream cheese, cut in chunks

1/3 cup mayonnaise

4 oz grated

cheddar cheese (or smoked gouda works well)

2/3 cup crabmeat *(Can vary the recipe with bay shrimp or chopped mushroom for the filling)*

2 tsp Old Bay seasoning

1 tsp fresh lemon juice

1/2 tsp Essence of Emeril seasoning or something similar

Elliott House
PO Box 297
Shaver Lake, CA
559-841-8601
www.elliotthouseandb.com
elliotthouse@psnw.com

INSTRUCTIONS:

Heat oven to 350 degrees. Lightly spray 12 small muffin cups. Melt 1 tablespoon of butter and lightly brush each wonton pastry before pushing into muffin cups.

Sauté green onions. Melt cheeses and mayonnaise in pan. Add seasonings and lemon juice. Add filling (could be crab, shrimp, mushrooms) to heat only. Scoop into wonton cups. Bake 12–15 minutes until wontons are golden brown.

COOK TIME: *1 dozen*
YIELD: *16 servings*

TWO MEETING STREET INN B&B

Charleston Chutney Cheese Appetizer

INSTRUCTIONS:
Mix all ingredients together. Refrigerate overnight. Excellent served with ginger snaps.

During the fall and holiday season, we like to use cranberry chutney. This spread is also an interesting accompaniment to pork and turkey.

This spread starts as a light beige color but after several hours it will darken to a golden yellow.

NOTE: *This very unique appetizer is great with water crackers, but even better with ginger snaps! We often double the recipe in order to have leftovers that would be great as a spread on turkey sandwiches after Thanksgiving instead of mayo.*

YIELD: *18 servings*

INGREDIENTS:

2 (8-oz) packages cream cheese

1/2 cup mango chutney

2 tsp curry powder

1 tsp dry mustard

Two Meeting Street Inn B&B
2 Meeting St
Charleston, SC
843-723-7322
www.twomeetingstreet.com
innkeeper2meetst@bellsouth.net

You don't have to be an angel, just be someone who can give.

PATTI LABELLE

Alluring Appetizers

GREY GABLES B&B

Caper Puffs

INGREDIENTS:

1 tsp capers

1¼ cups mayonnaise

1½ cups sharp cheddar cheese, shredded

6 green onions, finely chopped

1 package English muffins

INSTRUCTIONS:
Put capers between waxed paper and mash. Mix mayonnaise and cheese. Add onions and capers. Quarter English muffins and spread with mixture. Broil 3 minutes or until bubbly.

COOK TIME: *5 min*
YIELD: *10 or more servings*

Grey Gables B&B
PO Box 52
Rugby, TN
423-628-5252
www.rugbytn.com
greygablestn@highland.net

PROSPECT HILL PLANTATION INN & RESTAURANT

Chocolate Chip Pumpkin Bread

INGREDIENTS:

1 lb fresh crab meat, picked over to remove any shell bits

2 eggs

1/2 cup cooked & pureed squash

3 scallions, chopped

1/2 cup cracker crumbs

1 tbsp Old Bay Seasoning

1 tbsp lemon juice

7 sheets phyllo dough

non-stick cooking spray (or melted butter)

1/4 cup ground pecans

1/2 cup shredded Parmesan cheese

INSTRUCTIONS:

Preheat oven to 350 degrees F and grease a 15×12-inch cookie sheet.

Combine crab, eggs, pureed squash, scallions, cracker crumbs, Old Bay seasoning and lemon juice. Set aside.

Separate first sheet of phyllo and lightly spray or butter. Sprinkle with Parmesan and cover with second sheet of phyllo. Spray and sprinkle with nuts. Alternate cheese and nuts for remaining sheets. Mold crab mixture in a row on the long edge facing you. Roll all seven sheets to form a tube around crab. Transfer to pregreased pan. Bake at 350 degrees F 15 to 20 minutes or until golden brown. Cut into 1-inch strudel rolls.

COOK TIME: *20 min*
YIELD: *6 servings*

Prospect Hill Plantation Inn & Restaurant
PO Box 6909
Charlottesville, VA
540-967-0844
www.prospecthill.com
info@prospecthill.com

Alluring Appetizers

FAIRVIEW INN

Crab Cakes with Charred Corn,

INGREDIENTS:

Crab Cakes:

1 lb crab meat, lump

1/4 cup mayonnaise

1 egg, beaten

1 tbsp Creole mustard

1 tbsp lemon juice, fresh

2 tsp Old Bay Seasoning

1 tbsp cilantro, minced

1 tsp garlic, minced

2 tsp shallots, finely chopped

1 tbsp horseradish

2 tbsp yellow & red bell pepper, diced

dash of hot sauce

salt & pepper to taste

panko bread crumbs to bind about 1/2 cup or more

INSTRUCTIONS:

Crab Cakes: Mix everything in a large stainless steel bowl, except for breadcrumbs. Add the panko last. Form into 4 ounce cakes; lightly dredge in cornmeal and saute, with a little olive oil over medium heat. Brown on each side and finish in the oven at 400 degrees F for 5 minutes.

Inn Love

Tomato Salsa, and Poblano Aioli

Charred Corn and Tomato Salsa: Shuck and clean the corn, roast the corn over an open flame (gas stovetop, grill, etc.) Place the corn into a ziplock bag to "sweat" for 30 minutes. In the meantime mix the remaining ingredients in a stainless steel bowl. Scrape the corn off the cob with a knife, add the corn to the tomato mixture and mix well.

Poblano Aioli: Prepare the peppers the same as the corn. Peel the skins off the peppers and place in a food processor, along with remaining ingredients and pulse until smooth.

Place the corn relish around a small plate, place some baby spinach in the middle of the plate and the crab cake on top of the spinach. Place 1 tablespoon of aioli on top of crab cake.

COOK TIME: *35 min*
YIELD: *4 servings*

Fairview Inn
734 Fairview St
Jackson, MS
601-948-3429
www.fairviewinn.com
fairview@fairviewinn.com

Charred Corn and Tomato Salsa:

4 ears of yellow sweet corn

1 cup Roma tomatoes, diced

1 shallot, small dice

1 tsp garlic, minced

2 tsp apple cider vinegar

2 tbsp olive oil

2 tbsp cilantro, chopped

salt and pepper to taste

Poblano Aioli:

2 poblano peppers

1 tbsp lime juice

1 tbsp garlic

1 tbsp shallots

2 tbsp cilantro

2 cup mayonnaise

salt and pepper

Alluring Appetizers

The Main Squeeze

THE ONLY THING BETTER than a dinner out with your sweetheat is sharing a dinner in with them. Impress your lover with an extravagant meal while keeping the fireplace burning at home. Relax with a glass of wine, soft music, and the joy of knowing that the meal of your dreams came from your own two hands. Try any of these innkeeper favorites from the comforts of your dining room. From seafood risotto to roasted pork loin, any of these recipes are sure to be a hit with the one you love!

Find me a man who's interesting enough to have dinner with and I'll be happy.

LAUREN BACALL

TRANQUILITY BASE

Shirley's Stuffed Pork Loin with

INGREDIENTS:

For the stuffing:

2 slices dried bread, diced or broken

6 to 7 dried apricots, slivered

1½ tbsp (22 mL) finely chopped onion

1/8 tsp (0.5 mL) poultry seasoning

For the pork:

2 pork tenderloins

1 clove garlic

extra virgin olive oil, for brushing

1/2 cup (125 mL) chutney (try peach and red pepper)

Tranquility Base
110 Abbey Close
Ancaster, ON
905-648-1506
www.tranquilitybase.on.ca
tranquilitybnb@cogeco.ca

INSTRUCTIONS:

Combine stuffing ingredients and moisten with 1 tablespoon (15 mL) warm water. Set aside.

Butterfly pork by slicing tenderloins almost in half lengthwise and opening them up flat. Spread stuffing along length of one flattened tenderloin. Reverse second tenderloin and place on top of stuffing. Tie the 2 pieces together tightly about every 2 inches (5 cm), keeping stuffing tucked in on sides and ends. Cut garlic clove in half and rub over both sides of meat. Brush meat with oil on all sides. Allow to sit in fridge for at least 1 hour.

Bake in preheated oven at 375 degrees F (190 C) for about 1 hour. Check for doneness. Pork should be cooked to 150 to 165 degrees F (65 to 73 C). Remove from oven, cut into slices and arrange on a platter. Heat chutney and pour over pork. Serve immediately.

COOK TIME: *1 hr*
YIELD: *6 servings*

Chutney

Love is the joy of the good, the wonder of the wise, the amazement of the Gods.

PLATO

THE INN AT HONEY RUN

Seared Duck with Risotto and

INGREDIENTS:

4 each duck breasts, trimmed and scored

Kosher salt and cracked black pepper, to taste.

For the Brussels Sprouts:

1½ cup Brussels sprouts, cut in half

2 strips smoked bacon, diced

2 oz yellow onion, diced

2 oz celery, diced

1 garlic clove, minced

1 medium-sized carrot, cut into julienne strips (2" long × 1/8" wide)

1 bay leaf

2 sprigs fresh thyme

2 cup chicken broth

2 tbsp whole butter

black pepper to taste

INSTRUCTIONS:

For the duck: 4 each duck breasts, trimmed and scored *(ask you butcher to trim the breasts and score the skin; this will allow excess fat to render out of the duck and help create a crisp skin)*. Season the breasts heavily with the salt and pepper on both sides. Place the breast skin side down in a heavy bottomed sauté pan or cast iron skillet. Place over medium heat and slowly brown, removing excess fat as needed. Once the skin is crispy (about 8 minutes), turn the breast over and cook for another 4 minutes over low heat. Remove the cooked breasts to a cutting board and allow them to rest for 5 minutes before slicing.

NOTE: *Allowing the meat to rest will allow the juices to redistribute throughout the breast which will keep it moist for service.*

For the Brussels Sprouts: Place a small sauce pot over medium heat. Sauté the bacon, onion, garlic and celery together until the fat has rendered out of the breast and the vegetables are translucent. Place the Brussels sprouts and carrots into the pot along with the herbs and broth. Cover the pot and simmer until the sprouts are tender (about 12 minutes). Remove the bay leaf and thyme sprigs. Swirl in the whole butter and season as needed with the pepper.

Inn Love

Brussels Sprouts

For the Risotto: Place a small sauce pot over medium heat. Add the butter and olive oil. Add the rice and toss in the fat. (This is an important step in that it prepares the rice to absorb the broth and gives the rice a toasted flavor.) Add the diced butternut squash. Slowly add the stock 1/2 cup at a time and stir the rice constantly until the liquid is absorbed. (This gives risotto its texture and creaminess by releasing starches.) Repeat this step until all of the liquid is absorbed or the rice is cooked. Fold in the mascarpone, season to taste with the salt, pepper and asiago.

For the Risotto:

1 cup Arborio or carnoli rice

3 cup warm chicken broth

2 cloves garlic, minced

1/2 cup raw butternut squash, diced small

1 oz onion, diced

2 oz mascarpone cheese

1 tsp whole butter

1 tsp olive oil

Kosher salt and cracked pepper to taste

Grated asiago cheese to taste

The Inn at Honey Run
6920 Country Rd #203
Millersburg, OH
330-674-0011
www.innathoneyrun.com
info@innathoneyrun.com

The Main Squeeze

PASFIELD HOUSE INN

Chicken with Five Herb Cream

INGREDIENTS:

4 (8-oz) boneless skinless chicken breasts, halved and trimmed

1/4 bunch fresh parsley

about 6 fresh sage leaves

1 large sprig fresh rosemary

2 sprigs fresh thyme

about 8 fresh sweet basil leaves

1 pint heavy cream

1 cup white cooking wine *(preferably Chablis or chardonnay)*

1/4 cup chicken stock

Kosher salt

white pepper

nutmeg

2 tbsp sweet butter

A traditional French recipe in the "payson" or "country" style used in Southern France.

INSTRUCTIONS:

Rinse chicken breasts and lay out on a flat surface between two sheets of plastic film wrap. Using the flat side of a meat mallet, pound the chicken to uniform thickness. Season with salt and pepper and set aside.

Remove the rosemary and thyme leaves from the stems and discard stems. Finely chop all of the herbs together.

Heat a large sauté pan over medium high heat. Add the butter, and when it slightly browns, lay the chicken pieces flat in the pan. Cook until you achieve a slight sear on both sides of the chicken, turning the pieces only once (about 1 minute per side). Turn the heat up to high and add about half of the wine.

Using a wooden spoon for a non-stick pan or steel tongs for a shiny metal pan; deglaze the pan loosening all of the browned bits from the pan's cooking surface. Add the chicken stock, heavy cream and half of the chopped herbs and bring to a boil. Continue to reduce the sauce until slightly larger bubbles begin to form.

Sauce

Add the remaining herbs and half of the remaining wine. The reserved wine can be used to correct the sauce if it becomes too thick. There's no need to remove the chicken – it will only become more tender and flavorful as the sauce cooks. Continue to reduce the sauce until it thickens. A good way to tell is when larger bubbles form and the sauce starts to pull away from the edges of the pan. Season the chicken with salt, white pepper and nutmeg to taste. Plate and serve by spooning the sauce over the chicken fillets.

YIELD: *4 servings*

> *Love is an irresistible desire to be irresistibly desired.*
>
> ROBERT FROST

Pasfield House Inn
525 S. Pasfield St
Springfield, IL
217-525-3663
www.pasfieldhouse.com
innkeeper@pasfieldhouse.com

The Main Squeeze

HISTORIC SAND ROCK FARM

Ahi Tuna Provencal

INGREDIENTS:

1 fennel root

salt & pepper

1/4 cup black niçoise olives

1/4 cup green olives

1/4 cup sun-dried tomatoes

1 lemon

1 orange

1/2 lb Ahi tuna

extra virgin olive oil

2 tbsp fresh basil, chopped

24 thick potato chips

1/8 cup chopped chives

INSTRUCTIONS:

Remove the greens from the fennel, and dice into 1/8 inch cubes. Saute over medium-high with olive oil, salt, and pepper until just translucent and tender. Pit the olives – place a small handful on the cutting board and firmly press them with the back of a sauté pan, move the pan and press until you feel the pits. Rough chop. If sun-dried tomatoes are dry, rehydrate; if in oil, drain oil. Rough chop. Peel strips of orange and lemon zest with a sharp carrot peeler, and then dice the zest; make 1 teaspoon each of orange and lemon zest. Dice the tuna into 1/8-inch cubes. Combine tuna, zest, olives, tomatoes, fennel and 2 tablespoons olive oil with basil, salt and pepper to taste. Spoon a small heaping mound of the tuna mixture onto each chip. Sprinkle with chives.

This recipe is courtesy of Sand Rock Farm's Chef/Proprietor Lynn Sheehan

Historic Sand Rock Farm
6901 Freedom Blvd
Aptos, CA
831-688-8005
www.sandrockfarm.com
reservations@sandrockfarm.com

CHESTNUT STREET INN
Seafood Risotto

INSTRUCTIONS:

Heat olive oil and butter in a large sauté pan over medium high heat. Add onion. Sauté for approximately 5 minutes or until soft and translucent. Add garlic and sauté for a minute or until fragrant. Add carrots and celery. Sauté for a couple of minutes. Add bay leaf, Italian seasoning, salt and pepper and tomato paste. Sauté for a minute or two until fragrant.

Add rice and toast for just a minute to coat rice with oil and butter. Deglaze the pan with vermouth. Bring to a boil. Reduce heat to a simmer and cook uncovered until all the liquid has evaporated. Continue adding a ladle full of hot chicken broth to the mixture at a time, stirring constantly until all the liquid has evaporated, until the rice is tender, but still al dente.

Add shrimp and scallops and cook another 5 minutes or so until the shrimp and scallops are just cooked through, but not rubbery. Add parsley and freshly grated cheese and season to taste. Serve immediately.

COOK TIME: *45 min*
YIELD: *5 servings*

Chestnut Street Inn
PO Box 25
Sheffield, IL
815-454-2419
www.chestnut-inn.com
monikaandjeff@chestnut-inn.com

INGREDIENTS:

1 onion, chopped

1 carrot, peeled and chopped

1 celery stalk, chopped

2–3 garlic cloves, minced

1 bay leaf

1 tbsp Italian seasoning

pinch salt and pepper

2–3 tbsp olive oil

2 tbsp unsalted Butter

2 tbsp tomato paste

1/2 cup dry vermouth or dry sherry

1½ cups Arborio rice

1 bunch Italian parsley, finely chopped

3–4 cups hot chicken broth

1/2 lb shrimp, peeled and deveined

1/2 lb sea scallops

freshly grated Parmesan or Pecorino Romano cheese

The Main Squeeze

FRYEMONT INN

Trout Hugo

INGREDIENTS:

4 (6-oz) trout fillets, dredged in flour

1/4 cup butter

1/4 lb mushrooms

1 tbsp flour

3/4 cup white wine

1/4 cup chicken broth

chopped parsley for garnish

Fryemont Inn
PO Box 459
Bryson City, NC
828-488-2159
www.fryemontinn.com
fryemont@dnet.net

INSTRUCTIONS:

Melt butter in a large skillet. Add floured trout fillets, skin side up, and sauté over medium heat until golden brown, about 5 minutes. Flip over and continue cooking until center is opaque and fillets are cooked through about 1 minute more. Remove to a heated platter and keep warm while preparing sauce.

Add sliced mushrooms to pan drippings, adding a little more butter if necessary. Sauté 2 minutes. Sprinkle flour over the top and stir. Add the wine and broth and mixing well, bring it to a gentle boil. When entire surface is bubbly, sauce is done. Spool over the warm trout.

Garnish with chopped parsley and serve.

COOK TIME: *10 min*
YIELD: *4 servings*

Flowers always make people better, happier, and more helpful; they are sunshine, food and medicine for the soul.

LUTHER BURBANK

Sweet Nothings

NO MATTER HOW DELICIOUS or filling any meal may be, there's always room for dessert. Whether the sun or the moon hangs in the sky, these delectable sweets add the perfect finish to any romantic meal. Celebrating an anniversary or a first date? Reach for a recipe that will charm and seduce that special someone. Hosting a party? Pull a page from the innkeepers who bake the best, and put together a platter of cookies, pies, cakes and more for your guests to enjoy. Seeking a snack? Pick your favorite treat and create a quick pick me up that will last for days to come. Relish in the sweet nothings that bring you and your loved ones close.

To love abundantly is to live abundantly, and to love forever is to live forever.

HENRY DRUMMOND

BLACK CAT GUEST RANCH

Saskatoon Pie

INGREDIENTS:

4 cups Saskatoon berries

1/2 cup fruit juice (raspberry or orange)

1 cup sugar

3 tbsp flour

dash of salt

dash of nutmeg

1 tbsp butter

INSTRUCTIONS:

Mix berries and juice in large bowl. Mix sugar, flour, salt and nutmeg and mix into the berries. Pour into unbaked 9-inch pie shell. Dot with butter. Cover with top crust that has small holes cut into it with thimble. Seal edges well, baste top with cream and sprinkle with sugar. Bake at 425 degrees F for 15 minutes. Reduce oven to 350 degrees F and bake until nicely browned and juice begins to bubble through holes.

YIELD: *6 servings*

Black Cat Guest Ranch
PO Box 6267
Hinton, AB
780-865-3084
www.blackcatguestranch.ca
Perry@blackcatguestranch.ca

CLAY CORNER INN

Raspberry Walnut Torte

INGREDIENTS:

1/2 cup sugar

1 egg

1 cup softened butter

1 tsp vanilla

2 3/4 cups flour

1 tsp. baking powder

1/8 tsp. salt

1 cup raspberry preserves

1 cup chopped walnuts

2 tsp grated lemon peel

INSTRUCTIONS:

Mix sugar and egg; add butter and beat until smooth. Add vanilla, flour, baking powder and salt, mixing just until combined. Divide dough in half, wrap each ball with plastic wrap and refrigerate at least an hour. Take out one half and press into a greased 10-inch springform pan.

Mix together raspberry preserves, walnuts and lemon peel. Spread this mixture over the dough, then with a cheese grater, grate the other dough half evenly over the raspberry blend. Bake about 45 minutes in a 350 degree F oven. Cool on wire rack before removing sides. Enjoy.

NOTE: *Short, buttery, crunchy, delicious any time of day. Looks lovely, freezes well. Plan ahead as dough is refrigerated a couple hours before assembling and baking in a 10-inch springform pan.*

YIELD: *12 servings*

Clay Corner Inn
401 Clay Street SW
Blacksburg, VA
540-552-4030
claycorner.com
stay@claycorner.com

SEYMOUR LAKE LODGE

Sumptuous Apple Crisp

INGREDIENTS:

1/4 lb butter

1 cup sugar

1 tsp vanilla

1 egg

1 cup flour

1/4 tsp salt

1 tsp baking soda

1/2 cup white raisins

1 cup pecans, chopped

1/2 cup coconut

2 cups Granny Smith apples, chopped

Seymour Lake Lodge

28 Valley Rd

Morgan, VT

802-895-2752

www.seymourlakelodge.com

brianandjoan@comcast.net

INSTRUCTIONS:

Cream butter and sugar. Combine beaten egg and vanilla and add to butter mixture. Sift dry ingredients and add. Then stir in raisins, nuts and coconut. Add apples last. Bake in an 8½-inch square dish for 40 minutes at 350 degrees F. Serve warm with a scoop of vanilla ice cream.

Served in front of a flaming fire at Seymour Lake Lodge!

STILLMEADOW AT HAMPSTEAD

Apple Cranberry Crisp

INSTRUCTIONS:
Combine first 4 ingredients and pour into 13×9-inch baking dish. Combine remaining ingredients and pour over apple mixture. Press with spoon to smooth and bake for 30–40 minutes at 375 degrees F.

YIELD: 6 *servings*

INGREDIENTS:

- 6 medium apples (peeled and sliced)
- 1 can whole berry cranberry sauce (or we use 1 cup fresh cranberries, when in season)
- 3/4 cup sugar
- 2 tbsp flour

- 1/4 cup walnuts
- 1 cup rolled oats
- 1/2 cup brown sugar
- 1/2 cup flour
- 1 tsp cinnamon
- 1/4 cup melted butter

Stillmeadow at Hampstead
545 Main St
Hampstead, NH
603-329-8381
www.still-meadow.com
margaret.mitchell@still-meadow.com

Sweet Nothings

THE DUKE MANSION

Strawberry Bavarian Charlotte

INGREDIENTS:

For the Genoise:

8 eggs

9 oz sugar

1 tbsp vanilla

10 oz self rising flour

3 oz butter

Step one:

16 oz heavy cream

4 egg yolks

4 oz sugar

3 tbsp corn starch

Step two:

16 oz heavy cream

4 oz 10× fine sugar

3 gelatin sheets

3 oz warm water

4 oz strawberry puree

INSTRUCTIONS:

Combine eggs, sugar and vanilla in a stainless steel bowl and whisk. Heat over a double boiler until it reaches 110 degrees, constantly whisking. Have a 9-inch spring form pan greased with butter and floured and a baker's sheet tray greased and floured. When the egg mixture becomes 110 degrees, light and fluffy remove it from heat and lightly fold in the flour and the melted butter with a rubber spatula. Pour half the mixture into the spring form pan and the other half into the bakers sheet tray. With a metal spatula spread the batter over the length of the sheet tray. Place in an oven pre-heated to 350 degrees. Cook for 22 to 25 minutes or until a tooth pick comes out clean. The sheet tray should take about 12–14 minutes to fully cook. Remove from oven and allow to cool.

For the Strawberry Bavarian Cream: In a stainless steel bowl whisk together egg yolks, sugar and corn starch. In a separate sauce pan bring heavy cream to a boil. Temper egg yolks by mixing one third of hot cream to egg mixture slowly. Then reduce heat and add egg mixture into hot cream and slowly cook until it thickens. Cool over ice water bath.

In a stainless steel bowl whisk together sugar and heavy cream to soft peaks, not to stiff. Soften gelatin in warm water until dissolved. Add gelatin mixture to heavy cream mixture slowly until its incorporated. At last fold in berry puree and refrigerate.

When step one and step two are cooled and set, gently fold together by adding one third of step one mixture to step two mixture. Repeat until all is folded together.

To assemble: Cut 2 pieces of sheet tray cake 5" tall by 15" in length. Cut the sponge cake in half. Begin by laying the bottom piece of the sponge cake in a 9-inch spring form pan. Second step is to line the sides of the pan with the strips of sheet tray cake. Brush all inside exposed cake with the chocolate coating. Refrigerate and let set-up. Remove from refrigerator and fill partially with one third of Bavarian. Top with half sliced strawberries. Repeat the process starting with the cake, chocolate coating, Bavarian and strawberries. Finish by spreading remaining Bavarian on top of cake. Garnish with strawberry puree. Refrigerate until set, one hour. Remove from refrigerator and release the spring form and slice desired portion.

Remaining ingredients:

2 pints fresh strawberries, sliced

1 lb chocolate bar coating *(Find at specialty food stores. Soften chocolate by warming over a double boiler)*

2 oz strawberry puree

The Duke Mansion
400 Hermitage Rd
Charlotte, NC
704-714-4400
www.dukemansion.com
frontdesk@dukemansion.org

Sweet Nothings

1851 HISTORIC MAPLE HILL MANOR B&B

Bourbon Pecan Pie

INGREDIENTS:

1 cup sugar

3 tbsp butter, melted

1/2 cup dark corn syrup

3 large eggs, beaten

1½ to 2 cups pecan halves

2 tbsp good-quality bourbon

1 (9-inch) deep-dish pie shell, unbaked

INSTRUCTIONS:
Preheat the oven to 375 degrees F.

In a medium bowl, stir together the sugar and melted butter. Add the corn syrup, eggs, pecans and bourbon and stir until all ingredients are combined. Pour mixture into an unbaked pie shell, and place on a heavy-duty cookie sheet. Bake for 10 minutes. Lower the oven temperature to 350 degrees F, and continue to bake for an additional 25 minutes or until pie is set. Remove from oven and cool on a wire rack.

COOK TIME: *35 min*
YIELD: *8 servings*

1851 Historic Maple Hill Manor B&B

2941 Perryville Rd

Springfield, KY

859-336-3075

www.maplehillmanor.com

maplehillmanorbb@aol.com

CAMELLIA INN
Rhubarb Torte

INSTRUCTIONS:
Heat oven to 350 degrees F.

Grease an 11×15-inch baking pan or casserole. In food processor, process flour, powdered sugar and butter until it starts to come together, approximately 1 minute. Press into bottom of pan and bake for 20 minutes. Dice rhubarb. Process sugar, eggs, vanilla and salt until thick. Add flour and process 10 seconds. Stir into rhubarb and spread over crust. Bake until top is brown and firm, 35 minutes. Cool completely before serving. Cut into squares.

YIELD: *2 dozen*

INGREDIENTS:

1½ cups flour

4 tbsp powder sugar

2¼ cups sugar

1 tbsp vanilla

4 tbsp flour

3/4 cup butter (cut in pieces)

5 large stalks rhubarb (about 3 cups diced)

4 eggs

1/4 tsp salt

Camellia Inn
211 North St
Healdsburg, CA
707-433-8182
www.camelliainn.com
info@camelliainn.com

Sweet Nothings

THE EDGE OF THYME, A B&B INN

Gifford Family Tart

INGREDIENTS:

Cream together in food processor:

1¼ cups flour

1/4 cup sugar

1/4 lb butter

Add and process again:

1 tsp vanilla (real)

1 egg yolk

Apricot Glaze:

1 cup apricots (dried & chopped)

1/2 cup water

1/2 cup sugar

1 teaspoon lemon juice

The Edge of Thyme, A B&B Inn
100 Main St
Hyde Park, VT 05655
(866) 800-6888
info@OneHundredMain.com
www.OneHundredMain.com

INSTRUCTIONS:
Preheat oven to 350 degrees F.

Combine ingredients until a smooth dough is formed. Press into tart pan, flute the edges. Place decoratively any fresh, fruit on top. Bake for 30 minutes.

When cool, put apricot glaze on top. For apricot glaze, boil down to syrup and spoon over tart. *(I use different fruits depending on the fresh fruit in season, often slices apples with blueberries or raspberries are used decoratively.)*

COOK TIME: *30 min*

WOODLAND COVE
Cherry-Berry on a Cloud

INGREDIENTS:
6 egg whites

1/2 tsp cream of tartar

1/4 tsp salt

1¾ cup sugar

Filling:

2 cups heavy cream

8 oz cream cheese (softened)

1 cup sugar

1 tsp vanilla

2 cups miniature marshmallows

21-oz can cherry pie filling

2 full cups strawberries

1 tsp lemon juice

INSTRUCTIONS:
Beat egg whites until foamy, add cream of tartar and salt, beat until stiff. Beat in sugar gradually. Spread into a 9×13-inch glass baking dish. Bake at 275 degrees F for 45 minutes or until golden brown. Turn off oven and leave it for at least 6 hours (overnight is best).

Whip heavy cream then fold into cream cheese with sugar and vanilla. Add mini marshmallows. Spread over meringue. When ready to serve, top with the berry layer (cherry pie filling, mixed with sliced strawberries and lemon juice).

COOK TIME: *6 hrs 45 min*
YIELD: *12 servings*

Woodland Cove
PO Box 791
Kingston, TN
865-717-3719
www.woodlandcovebb.com
info@woodlandcovebb.com

Sweet Nothings

KAILUA HAWAII SHEFFIELD HOUSE

Bread Pudding *with Sweet Bread*

INGREDIENTS:

6 cups Portuguese sweet bread or other left over white bread

about 4 eggs

1 or 2 cups milk

1 tsp salt

cinnamon to taste

optional: raisins, craisins or nuts

Kailua Hawaii Sheffield House
131 Kuulei Rd
Kailua, HI
808-262-0721
www.hawaiisheffieldhouse.com
rachel@hawaiisheffieldhouse.com

This is a recipe to use the left over bread in your refrigerator. We like to use Cinnamon Sensations Portuguese Sweet bread.

INSTRUCTIONS:

Spray 9×12-inch baking pan with Pam. Tear up left over cinnamon sweet bread and add to baking dish. Mix eggs milk, cinnamon and salt. Pour over sweet bread and bake until firm. Bake at 350 degrees F for about 35 minutes.

COOK TIME: *35 min*
YIELD: *6 servings*

THE WINDWARD HOUSE

Poached Peaches *with White Cheese Mousse*

INSTRUCTIONS:
Combine first 4 ingredients in large glass mixing bowl. Microwave on high for 10 minutes. Stir until sugar dissolves. Add peach halves to syrup and microwave on high for 4 minutes. Refrigerate covered overnight. Beat all ingredients together, cover and refrigerate.

When ready to serve, place peach halves on serving plate cut side up. Spoon mousse into the pit cavity and sprinkle with nutmeg.

INGREDIENTS:

3 cups water

1½ cups sugar

1/3 cup lemon juice

1 tbsp vanilla

6 medium peaches, halved and pitted

1/2 cup ricotta cheese

1/4 cup Neufchatel (low fat) cream cheese

3 tbsp confectioners' sugar

1½ tsp lemon rind

1/2 tsp vanilla

The Windward House
24 Jackson St
Cape May, NJ
609-884-3368
www.windwardhouseinn.com
info@windwardhouseinn.com

Sweet Nothings

THE INN AT GRAY'S LANDING

Strawberries with *Lemon Creme*

INGREDIENTS:

6–8 medium strawberries *(see notes)*

1/2 cup Greek or plain yogurt

1/2 cup sour cream

2-3 tbsp sugar, to taste

the juice and zest of one lemon *(see notes)*

INSTRUCTIONS:

Wash and quarter strawberries, divide between two pretty glasses *(I use Champagne glasses)*. Whisk together yogurt and sour cream, then add the sugar and lemon juice. Drizzle two tablespoons of the lemon crème over each glass of the strawberries.

Grate lemon zest over the crème right before serving.

NOTES: *For a romantic snack fill a regular champagne glass (not a flute) half full with lemon crème and place whole, stems on, strawberries in the crème. Add the zest and let the honeymooners share.*

I also sometimes add blueberries, blackberries, raspberries, peaches, pineapple, whatever is fresh and in season. I like this tart so I use three tbsp lemon juice per cup of the yogurt/sour cream mixture.

YIELD: *2 servings*

The Inn at Gray's Landing
401 S King St
Windsor, NC
252-794-2255
www.grayslanding.com
innkeepers@grayslanding.com

DRIPPING SPRINGS RESORT

Dipped Cornbread with *Fruit and Creme*

INGREDIENTS:

cornbread

2 eggs

3/4 cup milk, or more

heavy cream flavored with rum or rum extract

dried fruit, diced (may use apricots or cranberries)

honey

INSTRUCTIONS:

Make your favorite cornbread recipe or use packaged mix, either is fine. Bake it in greased loaf/bread pan. Cool and chill slightly. Slice in 1-inch slices.

Mix eggs and milk and put in a shallow wide dish like a pie plate. Use more milk as needed. Dip each slice of cornbread quickly in the mixture, like French toast, do not let it set or it will come apart. In a frying pan, use either oil or butter and oil, for flavor. Butter burns easy so not too much. When oil is hot, place a couple of slices leaving plenty of turning room, quickly brown on both sides and transfer to individual plates.

In each plate, put 2 tablespoons of a heavy cream flavored with rum or rum flavoring, and a sprinkle of diced dried fruit like cranberries and apricots. Then put the slice of cornbread on the plate, with a drizzle more cream. Top with a dollop of whipped cream with a drizzle of honey, serve immediately.

NOTE: *This recipe is beautiful when presented on individual plates.*

Dripping Springs Resort

37 Dripping Springs Lane
Estes Park, CO
970-586-3406
www.drippingsprings.com
drippingsprings@gmail.com

Sweet Nothings

INN ON RANDOLPH

Poached Peaches in Champagne

INGREDIENTS:

2 large ripe peaches, preferably white

2 cups dry Champagne

1/2 cup maple syrup

1/2 small vanilla bean

3 large strawberries

2 tbsp powdered sugar

1/4 medium lemon, squeezed for juice

1 cup whipped cream

2 large mint leaves for garnish

Inn on Randolph
411 Randolph St
Napa, CA
707-257-2886
www.innonrandolph.com
innonrandolph@aol.com

INSTRUCTIONS:
Make a very light incision all around peach skins. Plunge the peaches briefly into boiling water, then into cold water, and peel. Place in a swallow pan and douse with Champagne. Add the syrup and vanilla bean. Bring to a slow boil over low heat, and poach peaches at about 185 degrees F, but do not allow to boil. If peaches are very ripe, they will be poached after 5 minutes.

Place peaches and syrup in a cool place, but do not refrigerate. Drain peaches, reserving the poaching liquid. Wash strawberries, remove any leaves, and puree in a blender or food processor. Place in a bowl and stir sugar into the puree. Stir whipped cream into the strawberry puree and add lemon juice.

Serve on round plates, or in glass dishes or small bowls. Line the bottom of the dishes with strawberry cream and arrange the cooled, but not chilled, peaches on top. Garnish each peach with a mint sprig. Serve the chilled poaching liquid separately in a sauce boat.

YIELD: *2 servings*

3 OAKS COUNTRY B&B

Apple Dumplings

INSTRUCTIONS:
Heat oven to 375 degrees F.

In small bowl, mix 2 tablespoons sugar and 1 teaspoon cinnamon and set aside. Unroll dough; separate into 8 triangles. Sprinkle sugar mixture evenly over each; gently press in, flattening each triangle slightly.

Place apple slice on shortest side of each triangle; tuck in dough edges around apple slice. Roll up, starting at shortest side of triangle and rolling to opposite side; seal all seams. In a 9 inch glass baking dish or pie dish, place long side of 7 filled rolls, point side down, around outside edge of dish; place 1 in center. Bake 15 to 20 minutes or until golden brown.

Remove partially baked rolls from oven. In small bowl, mix all sauce ingredients with wire whisk until well blended; spoon evenly over rolls. Sprinkle with almonds an cinnamon. Return to oven; bake 13 to 18 minutes longer or until deep golden brown, covering with foil during last 5 minutes of baking if necessary to prevent excessive browning. Serve warm. Store leftovers in refrigerator.

COOK TIME: *35 min*
YIELD: *8 servings*

INGREDIENTS:

Wrapped Apples:

2 tbsp sugar

1 tsp cinnamon

1 can (8-oz) crescent dinner rolls

1 large apple, peeled, cut into 8 slices

Sauce:

1/2 cup sugar

1/2 cup whipping cream

1 tbsp almond extract

1 egg

Topping:

1/2 cup sliced almonds

cinnamon

3 Oaks Country B&B
10205 Devore Dr
Harrison, AR
870-743-4093
www.3oaksbb.com
relax@3oaksbb.com

Sweet Nothings

BLESSINGS ON STATE

Passionate Poached Pears in Raspberry Sauce

INGREDIENTS:

2 fresh pears

1 tbsp maple syrup

1 tbsp brown sugar

1/2 tsp cinnamon sugar mix

1 cup fresh or frozen raspberries

1/4 cup powdered confectioner's sugar

Sweet things happen. They still do.

DIANNE WIEST

INSTRUCTIONS:

Peel the pears and core them from the bottom, leaving the stem intact. Trim a thin slice from the bottom of each so that they will stand upright. Place them in a microwave-safe pie plate and drizzle them with the maple syrup. Sprinkle them with brown sugar, and then sprinkle with cinnamon. Cover tightly with plastic wrap and cook on high power until they are tender, but not mushy, 6–10 minutes, depending on ripeness.

Gently lift them out of the pie plate and place them in stemmed sherbet or Champagne glasses.

If using frozen raspberries, heat them in a saucepan until they're thawed. Place raspberries in a blender and puree until completely blended. Pour the raspberry mixture through a strainer, stirring and pressing to force the juices into a bowl while removing the seeds. Pour the syrup back into the pan and place over low heat. Stir in the confectioner's sugar, stirring until thickened. Pour the warm sauce over the raspberries and garnish with a mint leaf and fresh raspberries, if available.

COOK TIME: *10 min*
YIELD: *2 servings*

Blessings On State
1109 W State St
Jacksonville, IL
217-245-1013
www.blessingsonstate.com
innkeeper@blessingsonstate.com

154 *Inn Love*

KALTENBACH'S
Cherry Cheesecake

INSTRUCTIONS:
Pre-heat oven to 375 degrees F.

Combine flour and brown sugar in bowl. Cut in shortening until crumbly. Stir in half of the nuts and coconut. Reserve 1/2 cup of the mixture for the topping. Press remaining mixture into greased 9×13-inch baking pan. Bake for 15 minutes.

Beat cream cheese, sugar, eggs, and vanilla in mixer bowl until smooth. Spread over hot baked layer. Bake for 15 minutes.

Top with pie filling, spreading to edge.

Combine remaining nuts and reserved crumb mixture in a small bowl. Sprinkle over pie filling. Bake for 15 minutes. Let stand until cool. Chill in refrigerator.

YIELD: *9 servings*

INGREDIENTS:

1¼ cup flour

1/2 cup packed brown sugar

1/2 cup butter-flavored shortening

1 cup chopped walnuts, divided

1/2 cup flaked coconut

16 oz cream cheese, softened

2/3 cup sugar

2 eggs

2 tsp vanilla extract

2 (21-oz) cans cherry pie filling

Kaltenbach's
743 Stonyfork Rd
& Kelsey St
Wellsboro, PA
570-724-4954
www.kaltenbachsinn.com

Sweet Nothings

BELFRY INNE & BISTRO

Pumpkin Cheesecake

INGREDIENTS:

2 (8-oz) packages cream cheese

3/4 cup white sugar

1 (15-oz) can pumpkin puree

1¼ tsp ground cinnamon

1/2 tsp ground ginger

1/2 tsp ground nutmeg

2 eggs

1/4 tsp salt

8 (4-oz) baking cups

Belfry Inne & Bistro
PO Box 2211
Sandwich, MA
508-888-8550
www.belfryinn.com
info@belfryinn.com

INSTRUCTIONS:

Preheat oven to 350 degrees F (175 degrees C).

Beat together the cream cheese and the sugar; add the pumpkin and the spices. Beat in eggs one at a time and then add salt. Beat until creamy. Spray baking cups with non stick spray and pour the batter evenly into baking cups. Bake at 350 degrees F (175 degrees C) for 40 minutes or until a knife inserted in the center comes out clean. Let cool.

GARNISHES:

Cinnamon whipped cream: Whisk together 1 cup heavy cream with 1 tablespoon powdered sugar, 1 teaspoon cinnamon, 1 teaspoon vanilla extract.

Goat cheese sauce: Beat together until smooth 2 ounces soft goats cheese, 2 ounces heavy cream, 1/2 tablespoon honey, 1/2 tablespoon powdered sugar.

Puff pastry sticks: Cut frozen puff pastry into sticks, lay on sheet pan lined with parchment paper, brush with melted butter, sprinkle with powdered sugar, cinnamon and cocoa powder. Bake for 10 minutes at 350 degrees F.

Pistachio Tuile: Mix 1/2 cup melted butter, 3/4 cup sugar, 1/3 cup flour, 1 ounce orange juice. Spread on baking sheet line with a Silpat, sprinkle with crushed pistachios. Bake for 8 minutes at 400 degrees F.

YIELD: *8 servings*

CHESTNUT HILL B&B

Overnight Pear Souffle

INSTRUCTIONS:

Spread butter or margarine on both sides of bread (It is easier to do if bread is frozen.) With sharp knife, cut bread into 1-inch squares. Grease 8×8×2-inch pan. Place bread in pan. Combine eggs, milk, sugar, nutmeg, and salt, pour over bread. Cover and refrigerate overnight.

Following day: Cut pears as directed. Dip in lemon juice to retard discoloration. Place pear slices over bread mixture. Preheat oven to 325 degrees, F. Bake at 325 for 40 minutes, or until bread mixture sets. Sprinkle with cheese and bake 5 minutes longer or until cheese melts.

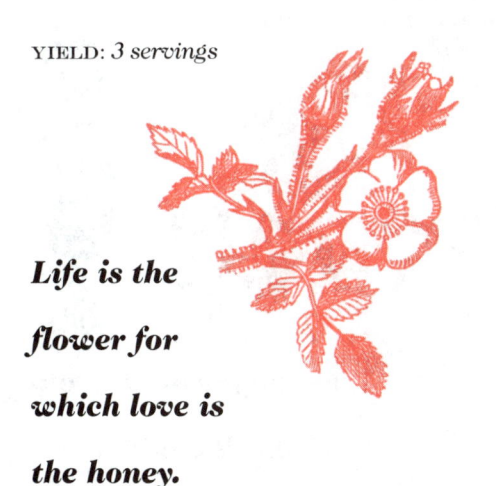

YIELD: *3 servings*

Life is the flower for which love is the honey.

VICTOR HUGO

INGREDIENTS:

3 tbsp butter or margarine

4 slices enriched white bread with crusts

3 eggs, beaten

1 cup evaporated skim milk

2 tsp sugar

1/8 tsp nutmeg

1/8 tsp salt

2 pears (Anjou or Bartlett), peeled, cored, and sliced

1 tbsp lemon juice

1/2 cup shredded low fat cheddar cheese or skim mozzarella cheese

Chestnut Hill B&B
236 Caroline St
Orange, VA
540-661-0430
www.chestnuthillbnb.com
kayers1214@aol.com

Sweet Nothings

BEAUFORT INN AND SOUTHERN GRACES BISTRO

Chocolate Crème Brulée

INGREDIENTS:

Chocolate crème brulee:

3/4 cup sugar

3 eggs

1½ cup milk

1/4 cup heavy cream

5 ounces melted bitter chocolate

Sweet basil vanilla sauce:

1/2 cup milk

1 cup basil leaves

1/4 cup sugar

1 cup heavy cream

1 vanilla bean, sliced

Beaufort Inn and Southern Graces Bistro
809 Port Republic St
Beaufort, SC
843-379-INNS (4667)
www.beaufortinn.com
julie.myers@beaufortinn.com

INSTRUCTIONS:

Brulee: Combine all ingredients, pour into 4-oz ramekins, bake in a water bath at 350 degrees F for approximately 50 minutes or until the center starts to gel. Refrigerate.

Vanilla sauce: Combine milk, basil and sugar in a Cuisinart blend until smooth. In a sauce pan bring together the blended mix with the cream and vanilla bring to a boil and then on a low flame reduce until sauce-like consistency. Take the vanilla bean out and spoon the seeds into the sauce. Chill and serve.

Take the brulee out of the cup sprinkle sugar on top and caramelize with the torch (propane flame) decorate with sauce.

Trust no friend without faults, and love a woman, but no angel.

DORIS LESSING

APPLEBROOK B&B
Apple Claflutti

INGREDIENTS:

Wet ingredients:

4 eggs

1 cup half & half

1 tsp vanilla

1/4 cup sugar

3 tbsp melted butter (cooled)

Dry ingredients:

1 cup all-purpose flour

1/4 tsp salt

Topping:

1 Granny Smith apple

cinnamon

sugar

2 tbsp melted butter

INSTRUCTIONS:
Preheat oven to 350 degrees F.

Mix wet ingredients. Add dry ingredient mix until no lumps. Spray a non-stick 8–12-inch skillet with cooking spray and pour in batter. Slice or use a mandolin to slice peeled apple thinly. Decoratively display apple on top of batter. Sprinkle with cinnamon and sugar. Drizzle with melted butter.

Bake for 20 minutes at 350 until puffs up and starts to brown.

OPTIONAL: *Serve sprinkled with powdered sugar and real maple syrup.*

COOK TIME: *20 min*
YIELD: *4 servings*

Applebrook B&B
Route 115A
Jefferson, NH
603-586-7713
www.applebrook.com
info@applebrook.com

Sweet Nothings

ROSEMARY HOUSE B&B

Pear Ginger Upside-Down Cake

INGREDIENTS:

1/2 stick unsalted butter, melted

1/4 cup light brown sugar, firmly packed

2 tbsp crystallized ginger, finely chopped, plus additional for garnish

2 tbsp currants or raisins

2 large Anjou pears, peeled, cored, and sliced thin

1 tbsp fresh lemon juice

1/2 cup all-purpose flour

1/2 tsp double-acting baking powder

1/4 tsp salt

1/2 tsp cinnamon

2 large eggs

1/4 cup plus 2 tbsp granulated sugar

1/2 tsp vanilla

whipped cream or vanilla ice cream as an accompaniment

INSTRUCTIONS:

Preheat oven to 400 degrees F.

Onto an 8-inch round cake pan pour the butter, swirling the pan, and sprinkle it with brown sugar, 2 tablespoons of the ginger, and the currants. In a small bowl toss the pear slices with the lemon juice and arrange them evenly over the currants. Into another small bowl sift together the flour, the baking powder, the salt, and the cinnamon. In a bowl with an electric mixer beat the eggs with the granulated sugar and the vanilla for 3 to 5 minutes, or until the mixture is thick and pale and forms a ribbon when the beaters are lifted. Fold in the flour mixture gently but thoroughly, pour the batter over the pear slices, and bake the cake for 20 to 25 minutes, or until a tester comes out clean. Run a sharp knife around the edge of the pan, invert the cake onto a serving plate, and serve it warm with the whipped cream or ice cream, sprinkled with remaining chopped crystallized ginger.

COOK TIME: *25 min*
YIELD: *6 servings*

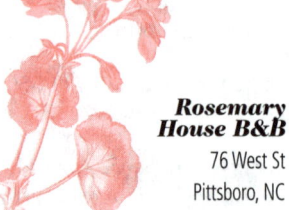

Rosemary House B&B
76 West St
Pittsboro, NC
919-542-5515
www.rosemary-bb.com
karen@rosemary-bb.com

SECOND WIND COUNTRY INN B&B

Camp Fire Pineapple Upside Down Cake

One of our favorite things to do here at Second Wind is a campfire. We even do morning campfires and this is an incredible breakfast to make on some red hot coals.

INSTRUCTIONS:
You will need a donuts, pineapple ring and square of tin foil for each upside down cake you make. Place donuts in middle of tin foil. Fill middle of donuts with a heaping tablespoon of brown sugar. Slice l tablespoon butter and place thin slices of it over top of donuts. Place pineapple ring on top. Wrap tin foil around it. Place on hot coals in fire. flip after a few minutes. Take off of coals and place on a paper plate, open, eat, and enjoy! They are wonderfully amazing.

INGREDIENTS:

sugar-cinnamon cake donuts from the bakery

canned pineapple rings

butter

brown sugar

Second Wind Country Inn B&B
30475 Carlson Road
Ashland, WI
715-682-1000
www.secondwindcountryinn.com
catchyourbreath@secondwindcountryinn.com

Sweet Nothings

CHANTICLEER INN

Almond Pear Clafouti

INGREDIENTS:

1/2 cup sugar

1 cup low-fat or whole milk

3 eggs

1 tsp vanilla extract

1 tsp almond extract

1/3 cup flour

1/3 cup almonds

2–4 pears, cored, peeled, and evenly sliced lengthwise (about 6 slices per pear).

1/2 cup cherries, pitted and halved

Chanticleer Inn
120 Gresham St
Ashland, OR
541-482-1919
www.ashland-bed-breakfast.com
comfy@ashlandbnb.com

INSTRUCTIONS:
In a blender combine all ingredients, except the pears and cherries. Blend very well, scraping the sides of the blender a few times to get all the flour mixed in and almonds ground.

Prepare the pears and arrange on the bottom of the greased pan in a pinwheel fashion, with the base of the pear sections toward the outer edge. Add the cherries in the center.

Slowly pour the egg batter into the pie pan – the pears will float so nudge them about to keep their pinwheel formation.

Bake in the oven until set, puffy and golden about 45-60 minutes. Cut into 6 slices.

NOTE: *Clafoutis (claw-foo-tea) are a traditional country French dessert, best described as a cross between a cake and flan. With the addition of ground almonds, I reduced the amount of flour. If you wish for more a cake texture, add 1/3 cup more flour.*

COOK TIME: *50 min*
YIELD: *2 servings*

162 *Inn Love*

OLD RED INN & COTTAGES
West Haven Cake

INSTRUCTIONS:
Preheat oven to 350 degrees F. Cream together sugar, shortening, eggs and vanilla. Set aside. Pour boiling water over dates and add baking soda. Sift together flour, salt and cocoa. Add flour mixture alternately with dates to shortening mixture. Spread mixture into 9×13-inch loaf pan or in a cake pan. Sprinkle with chocolate chips and ground nuts. Bake for 35 minutes. Sprinkle with confectioner sugar once it's done, while still warm. Cool and slice like cookie bars.

COOK TIME: *35 min*
YIELD: *16 servings*

INGREDIENTS:
1 cup sugar

2 eggs

1 cup boiling water

1 tsp baking soda

1/2 tsp salt

8 oz chocolate chips

1/2 cup shortening

1 tbsp vanilla

8-oz package of cut dates

1¾ cup flour

1 tsp cocoa

1/2 cup ground nuts

Old Red Inn & Cottages
PO Box 467
North Conway, NH
603-356-2642
www.oldredinn.com
OldRedInn@RoadRunner.com

BEAUMONT INN

Chocolate Sherry Cake

INGREDIENTS:

For cake:
10 eggs

1 cup white sugar

1/2 tsp vanilla

1⅝ cup flour

4 tsp cornstarch

1/4 cup butter, melted

2 tbsp shortening, to grease the cake pans

Chocolate Butter Cream Icing:

1 cup egg whites (about 8)

1 cup plus 1 tbsp sugar

1½ cup soft butter

1 tsp vanilla

3 oz sherry wine

2 squares melted chocolate or 3/4 cup cocoa

INSTRUCTIONS:

Make one 3-layer 9" sponge cake as follows:
Beat eggs and sugar in bowl over hot water until melted. Remove from hot water and continue beating until creamy and thick, approximately 10 minutes. Add vanilla. Sift flour and cornstarch together, and slowly and gently fold into mixture. Add melted butter slowly as you mix it slowly. Pour mixture equally into the 3 cake pans. Bake in preheated 350 degree oven for 25 minutes.

Chocolate Butter Cream Icing:
Mix egg whites and sugar; place over boiling water and stir slowly. When slightly warm, remove from heat and beat continuously for 7 minutes until stiff, or doubled in volume. Add vanilla and softened butter while beating 2 minutes or well blended. Store in refrigerator until cool but spreadable. When icing is ready, add 2 squares melted chocolate or 3/4 cup cocoa. Beat until well blended. Place one layer of cake on plate, sprinkle with 2 tablespoons sherry wine, spread icing, and repeat with next 2 layers. Be sure top and sides are heavily iced.

COOK TIME: *25 min*

Beaumont Inn
PO Box 158
Harrodsburg, KY
859-734-3381
http://www.beaumontinn.com
helen@beaumtoninn.com

LAUREL SPRINGS LODGE B&B

Zucchini Chocolate Cake

INSTRUCTIONS:
Cream together the butter, oil and sugar. Then add eggs, vanilla and buttermilk. Mix the cocoa, flour, baking powder, baking soda and salt, and then add to the wet ingredients. Mix well then stir in shredded zucchini, pour into a greased and floured 9×13-inch pan. Sprinkle with chocolate chips and chopped walnuts.

Bake at 325 degrees for 40 to 45 minutes.

COOK TIME: *45 min*
YIELD: *20 servings*

All you need is love. But a little chocolate now and then doesn't hurt.

CHARLES M. SCHULZ

INGREDIENTS:

1/2 cup butter

1/2 cup oil

1¾ cup sugar

2 eggs

1 tsp vanilla

1/2 cup buttermilk

4 tbsp cocoa

2½ cups flour

1/2 tsp baking powder

1 tsp baking soda

1 tsp salt

2 cups shredded zucchini

1 cup chocolate chips

1 cup chopped walnuts

Laurel Springs Lodge B&B
204 Hill St
Gatlinburg, TN
865-430-9211
www.laurelspringslodge.com
relax@laurelspringslodge.com

Sweet Nothings

ALOHA JUNCTION B&B INN

Bittersweet Chocolate Fondue

INGREDIENTS:

6 ounces (170 grams) semisweet or bittersweet chocolate, cut into small pieces

1/2 cup (120 ml) heavy whipping cream

1/4 cup (60 ml) milk

2½ tbsp (35 grams) granulated white sugar

2 tbsp light corn syrup

1 tsp pure vanilla extract

1/4 cup Nutella (optional)

1 tbsp Frangelico or other liqueurs such as Grand Marnier or brandy

Aloha Junction B&B Inn
PO Box 91
Volcano, HI
808-967-7289
www.bnbvolcano.com
alohajunction@hotmail.com

> *Life is short, and it is up to you to make it sweet.*
>
> SARAH LOUISE DELANY

INSTRUCTIONS:

Place the chopped chocolate in a medium sized stainless steel bowl and set aside.

Combine the cream, milk, sugar, and corn syrup in a saucepan and place over medium heat. Bring to a boil, stirring often.

Remove from heat and pour immediately over the chocolate. Let stand until the chocolate has melted, then whisk until smooth.

Whisk in vanilla extract, Nutella (if using), and alcohol.

Place the chocolate sauce in a fondue pot and serve with fresh fruits, chunks of pound, butter, sponge, or angel food cake and cookies (amaretti, ladyfingers, rolled wafer cookies, or biscotti).
Reheat the sauce if it becomes too thick.

Makes about 1½ cups.

YIELD: *4 servings*

1870 WEDGWOOD BED & BREAKFAST INN
Lemon Almond Biscotti

INSTRUCTIONS:
Preheat oven to 325 degrees.

Line a baking tray with parchment paper. Sift together first 4 ingredients. In a separate bowl, beat eggs and sugar until light in color. Beat in zest and lemon juice. Slowly add dry ingredients to the egg mixture. Add nuts. Turn dough onto lightly floured surface and knead until smooth, about 2 minutes. Do not overwork dough. Divide dough in half, shaping into 2 logs. Bake for about 30 minutes or until golden brown. remove from oven and allow to cool completely. Reduce oven to 300 degrees. Cut logs into 1/2-inch slices. Return to baking sheet and cook until toasted, about 20 to 30 minutes.

COOK TIME: *55 min*
YIELD: *2 dozen*

INGREDIENTS:

2½ cups all-purpose flour

1 tsp baking powder

1/2 tsp baking soda

1 tsp salt

4 large eggs

3/4 cup sugar

1 tbsp lemon zest

1½ tsp fresh lemon juice

1 cup almonds or Macadamia nuts, toasted

1870 Wedgwood Bed & Breakfast Inn of New Hope, PA

111 W Bridge St
New Hope, PA
215-862-2570
www.WedgwoodInn.com
stay@WedgwoodInn.com

Sweet Nothings

ACWORTH INN

Chocolate Mint Sticks

INGREDIENTS:

1/2 cup butter

2 oz unsweetened chocolate

1 cup sugar

1/4 tsp peppermint extract

2 large eggs

1/2 cup all-purpose flour, unsifted

pinch of salt

1/2 cup coarsely chopped toasted nuts (optional)

Icing:

2 tbsp butter, room temperature

3/4 tsp peppermint extract

1 cup confectioners' sugar, sifted

1 tbsp cream

Glaze:

1 tbsp butter

1 oz unsweetened chocolate

INSTRUCTIONS:

Line an 8-inch square pan with foil; lightly butter bottom and sides. In a double boiler or in a microwave, melt butter and chocolate. Stir in sugar and peppermint extract. Add beaten eggs, stirring until smooth. Add flour and salt; stir in nuts. Pour into prepared pan. Bake at 350 degrees F for 20–25 minutes. Cool. Lift brownies from pan by foil edges and frost.

Icing: Beat butter, peppermint, sugar and cream in a small bowl. Spread on brownies.

Glaze: In a double boiler or in a microwave, melt together the chocolate and butter. Drizzle this over the icing. Refrigerate till well-chilled. Cut into 3/4-inch × 2-inch sticks.

COOK TIME: *25 min*

Acworth Inn
PO Box 256
Cummaquid, MA
508-362-3330
www.acworthinn.com
acworthinn@acworthinn.com

COOL BREEZE B&B
Welsh Cakes

INSTRUCTIONS:

Measure first four ingredients into a large mixing bowl. Add butter. Mix well with a fork. Stir in currants or raisins. Break eggs into a small bowl. Beat until whites and yolks are well mixed. Stir milk and vanilla into the eggs. Add egg mixture to flour mixture until moist all the way through.

Dump the dough onto waxed paper or a pastry canvas that is sprinkled with a little flour. With your hands pat it out into a big circle about 1/4-inch thick. Use a large cookie cutter to cut it into as many cakes as you can.

Drop each onto a large griddle and cook just as you'd cook pancakes. When they're golden brown, they're done. On a cold winter evening, serve them with cups of hot chocolate or tea. Your family or guests will love them.

NOTE: *A guest from Ohio sent me this recipe and said that Welsh cakes are as traditional in Wales as fish and chips are in England. You cut them out, cook them like pancakes, and eat them like cookies. I like them plain or sometimes I include dried cranberries into the mixture. My guests like them very much.*

INGREDIENTS:

2 cups flour

1 cup dried currants/raisins *(optional)*

1 cup sugar

1/4 cup milk

1½ tsp baking powder

1/2 tsp nutmeg

1/2 tsp vanilla extract

2 eggs

3/4 cup softened butter

Cool Breeze B&B
1240 SE Second St
Evansville, IN
812-422-9635
www.coolbreezebb.net
coolbreeze27@juno.com

Sweet Nothings

ARTIST'S INN & GALLERY

Chocolate Melt-Away Cookies

INGREDIENTS:

3/4 cup soft butter

2 1/3 cups unbleached flour

1 cup sugar

2 eggs

1 tsp baking powder

1/2 tsp salt

1/2 tsp ground cinnamon

1/2 tsp almond extract

1 (6-oz) package semisweet chocolate pieces, about 1 cup

powdered sugar

INSTRUCTIONS:

In a large mixer bowl, beat butter. Add half of the flour, sugar, eggs, baking powder, salt, cinnamon and almond extract. Beat thoroughly. Beat in remaining flour. Divide dough in half. Cover, chill 1 hour or until firm.

On a lightly floured surface roll half of the dough 1/8-inch thick. The thinner you can roll the dough, the better these cookies will taste. Keep remaining dough in fridge until ready to use. Cut into shapes with 1½-inch to 2-inch cookie cutter (stars, rounds, hearts). Place on ungreased cookie sheets. With small cookie cutter, cut out centers from half of the unbaked cookies. Bake in a 375 degree F oven about 7 minutes or until edges are firm and bottoms are very light brown. Cool. Repeat with remaining dough. Melt chocolate pieces in a microwave at half power for about two minutes. Spread chocolate on bottom of each cookie. Top with cookie half that has the center cut in it. The chocolate will show through. When cool, dust with powdered sugar.

YIELD: *3 dozen*

Artist's Inn & Gallery
117 East Main Street
Terre Hill, PA
717-445-0219
www.artistinn.com
relax@artistinn.com

Inn Love

WHITE LACE INN

White Lace Inn Cookies

INGREDIENTS:

2 cup butter*

2 cup white sugar

2 cup brown sugar

4 eggs

3 tsp vanilla

4½ cup flour

2 tsp baking powder

2 tsp baking soda

8 cups* Quaker Oats Old Fashioned Oatmeal

1 (7-oz) Hershey Milk Chocolate Candy Bar, chopped into large pieces

3 Heath Candy Bars, chopped

1 cup nuts *(optional)*

INSTRUCTIONS:
Cream together butter, white sugar, and brown sugar. Beat in eggs and vanilla. Set aside. Mix together flour, baking powder, baking soda. Fold this into butter mixture. Add to this the oatmeal, candy bars, and nuts (if using nuts).

Make large cookies and bake in a preheated 375 degrees F oven for 8–10 minutes*

*NOTES: *We always use 1/2 butter & 1/2 margarine, which is equal to 2 sticks of each. Also, we often use 9–10 cups of oatmeal. It is best to under bake a little.*

YIELD: *4 dozen*

White Lace Inn
16 N 5th Ave
Sturgeon Bay, WI
920-743-1105
www.whitelaceinn.com
Romance@WhiteLaceInn.com

Sweet Nothings

BURR HOUSE

Sweet Treats

INGREDIENTS:

1 stick soft butter

1 cup brown sugar

2 eggs

1/2 cup flour

1 tsp vanilla

1 cup chopped pecans

Burr House
210 E Chestnut
Bloomington, IL
309-828-7686
www.burrhouse.com
burrhouse@hotmail.com

How sweet it is!

JACKIE GLEASON

INSTRUCTIONS:
Cream together the butter and sugar. Add eggs and vanilla, mix well. Blend in the flour, then mix in the pecans. Spray a 2 dozen mini-muffin pan with Pam and fill almost full. Bake for 15 minutes or until done at 375 degrees F.

COOK TIME: *15 min*
YIELD: *2 dozen*

Love and desire are the spirit's wings to great deeds.

JOHANN WOLFGANG VON GOETHE

ALPHABETICAL LISTING OF INNS AND B&BS

Index

1851 Historic Maple Hill Manor B&B, 144
1868 Crosby House, 20
1870 Wedgwood Bed & Breakfast Inn of New Hope, PA, 167
3 Oaks Country B&B, 153

A

Abbeymoore Manor, 14
Academy Street Inn, 77
Acworth Inn, 168
Adams Basin Inn, 100
A.G. Thomson House, 17
Albert Shafsky House B&B, 39
Alegria Oceanfront Inn & Cottages, 32
Aloha Junction B&B Inn, 166
Apple Blossom Inn, 82
Applebrook B&B, 159
Arroyo Vista Inn, 52
Artist's Inn & Gallery, 170
A TreeHouse B&B, 27
Avenue Hotel Bed and Breakfast, 21

B

B&B at Roseledge Herb Farm, 34
Barclay Cottage Bed and Breakfast, 90
Beaufort Inn and Southern Graces Bistro, 158
Beaumont Inn, 164
Belfry Inne & Bistro, 156
Big Bear Bed & Breakfast, 65
Black Cat Guest Ranch, 138
Black Walnut Guest House, 23

Blessings On State, 154
Bottger Mansion of Old Town, 83
Brazos Oaks B&B, 60
Burr House, 172
Buttonwood Inn, 45

C

Camellia Inn, 145
Cameo Rose Victorian Country Inn, 81
Canyon Ferry Mansion, 104
Cape Charles House B&B, 19
Carriage House B&B, 102
Carter House Inns & Restaurant 301, 50
Chanticleer Inn, 162
Chestnut Hill B&B, 157
Chestnut Street Inn, 133
Clay Corner Inn, 139
Cool Breeze B&B, 169
Creekside B&B, 97
Crimson Cottage Inn the Woods, 48
Crisanver House, 78
Crystal River Inn, 71

D

Desert Dove B&B, 55
Dripping Springs Resort, 151

E

Earlystown Manor, 54
Edelweiss Manor, 96
Ellery House, 46
Elliott House, 118

F

Fairlea Farm Bed and Breakfast, 64
Fairview Inn, 122
Fairville Inn, 66
Fitch Hill Inn, 25
Flowers and Thyme Bed & Breakfast, 29
Fryemont Inn, 134

G

Goodbread House, 87
Grady House Historic Bed & Breakfast, 56
Grand Living B&B, 110
Grey Gables B&B, 120

H

Harborside House, 38
Haydon Street Inn, 99
Hickory Bridge Farm, 112
Hill Farm Inn, 16
Historic Sand Rock Farm, 132
Holland Inn, 62
Holly Court Inn, 31
Holly Hill House B&B, 72

I

Inn at Bath, 51
Inn at Ellis River, 24
Inn at Valley Farms B&B & Cottages, 98
Inn on Randolph, 152
Ivy Creek Farm, 101

J

J. Paules' Fenn Inn, 89

K
Kailua Hawaii Sheffield House, 148
Kaltenbach's, 155

L
La Maison de Lucy, 103
Laurel Springs Lodge B&B, 165
Lodge at Sedona, 117
Loganberry Inn, 88
Lovelace Manor, 74

M
Maison Beliveau, 70
Maison LaVigne, 107
Mill Street Inn, 53

N
North Lodge on Oakland, 41

O
Oak Cove, 111
Old Monterey Inn, 85
Old Red Inn & Cottages, 163

P
Pasfield House Inn, 130
Pelican Cove Inn, 86
Pleasant Lake B&B, 91
Poolside Paradise B&B, 26
Prospect Hill Plantation Inn & Restaurant, 121

R
Red Bluff Cottage, 93
Rosemary House B&B, 160

S
Second Wind Country Inn B&B, 161
Seymour Lake Lodge, 140
Simply Bed and Bread, 49
Stillmeadow at Hampstead, 141
Stonehurst Place, 116

T
Tahoma Meadows B&B Cottages, 73
Talkeetna Roadhouse, 108
Tefft House Bed and Breakfast, 22
Ten Bits Ranch, 61
The Colonel Taylor Inn Bed & Breakfast, 92
The Duke Mansion, 142
The Edge of Thyme, A B&B Inn, 146
The Grange at Stag Hollow, 63
The Hurst House, 28
The Inn at Gray's Landing, 150
The Inn at Honey Run, 128
The Irish Inn, 109
The Maine Stay Inn, 106
The Mainstay Inn, 18
The Maria Atwood Inn, 15
The Richmond Victorian Inn, 30
The Settlers Inn at Bingham Park, 37
The Summer Inn B&B, 58
The Windward House, 149
The Wine Country Inn & Gardens, 47
Tidewater Inn, 84
Timmermann House B&B, 44
The Yellow House, 79
Tranquility Base, 126
Two Meeting Street Inn B&B, 119

V
Victorian House B&B, 59

W
Waianuhea B&B, 36
Ware Street Inn, 40
Warwick Valley Bed & Breakfast, 75
White Lace Inn, 171
Widow Kip's Country Inn, 76
Williamsburg Sampler B&B Inn, 80
Woodland Cove, 147

Do you

have to have

a reason for

loving?

BRIGITTE BARDOT